# Far from the Madding Crowd

A play

## Matthew White

Adapted from the novel by Thomas Hardy

Samuel French — London
New York - Toronto - Hollywood

822

© 1999 BY MATTHEW WHITE

Rights of Performance by Amateurs are controlled by Samuel French Ltd, 52 Fitzroy Street, London W1P 6JR, and they, or their authorized agents, issue licences to amateurs on payment of a fee. **It is an infringement of the Copyright to give any performance or public reading of the play before the fee has been paid and the licence issued.**

The Royalty Fee indicated below is subject to contract and subject to variation at the sole discretion of Samuel French Ltd.

Basic fee for each and every
performance by amateurs     Code M
in the British Isles

Basic fee for each and every
performance of the music    Code A
in the British Isles

**The publication of this play does not imply that it is necessarily available for performance by amateurs or professionals, either in the British Isles or Overseas. Amateurs and professionals considering a production are strongly advised in their own interests to apply to the appropriate agents for consent before starting rehearsals or booking a theatre or hall.**

ISBN 0 573 01767 0

Please see page iv for further copyright information.

# FAR FROM THE MADDING CROWD

First presented at the Watermill Theatre, Newbury, on 2nd September 1997, with the following cast:

| | |
|---|---|
| **Bathsheba Everdene** | Jacqueline Charlesworth |
| **Gabriel Oak** | Martin Ledwith |
| **William Boldwood** | Andrew Hesker |
| **Sergeant Francis Troy** | Jonathan Wrather |
| **Fanny Robin** | Amanda Tingle |
| **Lydia Smallbury (Liddy)/Mrs Hurst** | Angela Sims |
| **Joseph Poorgrass** | David Gilbrook |
| **Jan Coggan** | Tony Bell |

Directed by Matthew White
Designed by Meg Surrey
Lighting by Paule Constable

## COPYRIGHT INFORMATION

(See also page ii)

This play is fully protected under the Copyright Laws of the British Commonwealth of Nations, the United States of America and all countries of the Berne and Universal Copyright Conventions.

All rights including Stage, Motion Picture, Radio, Television, Public Reading, and Translation into Foreign Languages, are strictly reserved.

**No part of this publication may lawfully be reproduced in ANY form or by any means—photocopying, typescript, recording (including video-recording), manuscript, electronic, mechanical, or otherwise—or be transmitted or stored in a retrieval system, without prior permission.**

Licences for amateur performances are issued subject to the understanding that it shall be made clear in all advertising matter that the audience will witness an amateur performance; that the names of the authors of the plays shall be included on all programmes; and that the integrity of the authors' work will be preserved.

The Royalty Fee is subject to contract and subject to variation at the sole discretion of Samuel French Ltd.

In Theatres or Halls seating Four Hundred or more the fee will be subject to negotiation.

In Territories Overseas the fee quoted above may not apply. A fee will be quoted on application to our local authorized agent, or if there is no such agent, on application to Samuel French Ltd, London.

---

### VIDEO-RECORDING OF AMATEUR PRODUCTIONS

Please note that the copyright laws governing video-recording are extremely complex and that it should not be assumed that any play may be video-recorded for whatever purpose without first obtaining the permission of the appropriate agents. The fact that a play is published by Samuel French Ltd does not indicate that video rights are available or that Samuel French Ltd controls such rights.

# CHARACTERS

**Bathsheba Everdene**
**Gabriel Oak**
**William Boldwood**
**Sergeant Francis Troy**
**Fanny Robin**
**Lydia Smallbury (Liddy)**
**Mrs Hurst**
**Joseph Poorgrass**
**Jan Coggan**

The members of the cast may also take on a variety of minor parts

The action of the play takes place in various interior and exterior settings in Dorset

Time: 1840s

## STAGING "FAR FROM THE MADDING CROWD"

This adaptation of *Far from the Madding Crowd* was actually written with a specific venue in mind — the beautiful Watermill Theatre in Bagnor, an old converted mill set in the heart of the Berkshire countryside. In many ways this was the perfect setting for a story in which the lives of the protagonists are so often affected by their natural surroundings. The mere fact that the audience approached the theatre by way of a small, winding country road, and upon entering the auditorium could actually hear the muted sounds of the mill stream beneath their feet, no doubt contributed to the overall effect of the production.

I mention the suitability of the venue only because it influenced our decisions when it came to designing a set for this production. Clearly our specific location did much of the work for us, and for this reason we opted for a very simple design which would subtly evoke each particular change of scene without being overly intrusive. Because of this, scene changes were very speedy and the general flow of the story was maintained throughout.

The basic design for this production was as follows; there was a box set, with a raised wooden floor. There were entrances and windows on both the side walls, and at the back there was a split "barn door" entrance and a window. This back wall was actually partly solid, and partly made of gauze; when the gauze was lit from behind, the audience could see into an upper room. This was reached by a hidden staircase. The main acting area was used for both interior and exterior scenes and minimal set dressing was added where necessary. For example, Bathsheba's study was suggested by a small desk, a chair, and a bench, whilst for the shearing supper we used a long table, two benches and a large hanging branch. Lighting, of course, played a vital role, and helped create a very different atmosphere for each scene.

We found that the simplicity of the set, and its subtle suggestiveness, gave the audience just enough to "place" each scene and to give it atmosphere, without being too heavy-handed. In this way the acting area very easily transformed from a sheep paddock to a church porch, from a farmhouse parlour to the banks of a mill pond. Sound effects were also very helpful in creating the specific mood of each scene, and we also used music, some live and some recorded, to facilitate the smooth transition from one scene to the next. Two of the actors in our cast were also accomplished musicians, and they played a variety of different instruments throughout the play.

I have outlined our original design ideas simply to indicate how staging difficulties were overcome in the Watermill production of *Far from the Madding Crowd*. Subsequent directors will, of course, make different choices and find other inventive ways of telling the story. My stage directions are intended merely as a guide-line, and they are to be used or disregarded at the director's discretion.

## NOTE

The following words should be used by the Priest in the fantasy wedding sequence on p.51.

Requiem æternam dona eis, Domine, et lux perpetua luceat eis. Te decet hymnus, Deus in Sion, et tibi reddetur votum in Jerusalem. Exaudi orationem meam, ad te omnis caro veniet. Requiem æternam dona eis, Domine, et lux perpetua luceat eis. Kyrie eleison. Christe eleison. Kyrie eleison.

## MUSIC

*The Banks of Allan Water* is a folk song with a traditional tune. The music for *Great Things,* by James Clutton, can be found on pp. 74-75.

## ACKNOWLEDGEMENTS

With thanks to James Clutton, Jill Frazer and the original members of the cast.

Matthew White

# For Lindsey

" Love is, yea, a great thing
A great thing to me."

# ACT I
## Scene I

*A forest clearing. Late November*

*Darkness. A solo flute can be heard*

*The Lights slowly brighten to reveal a young woman, Bathsheba Everdene, in the middle of the clearing. She is admiring herself in the reflection of a hand-held mirror, and as the flute tune plays, there is perhaps the feeling that she is moving, or even dancing to the music*

*After a short time, the Lights in another area of the stage come up, revealing Gabriel Oak, holding a woman's hat and watching Bathsheba from a distance. As the melody comes to an end, the lighting over the whole scene brightens*

**Gabriel** I found a hat.
**Bathsheba** It is mine. It flew away in the wind last night.

*Gabriel hands the hat to Bathsheba*

Thank you. You are Farmer Oak, are you not?
**Gabriel** That or thereabouts.
**Bathsheba** A large farm?
**Gabriel** No, not large. A couple of hundred sheep, Miss, er … Miss, I don't know your name. I know your aunt's but not yours.
**Bathsheba** I would just as soon not tell it. You can enquire at my aunt's — she will tell you.
**Gabriel** My name is Gabriel. Gabriel Oak.
**Bathsheba** You seem fond of yours in speaking it so decisively, Gabriel Oak.
**Gabriel** You see, it is the only one I shall ever have, and I must make the most of it. Now as for you, miss, well, I should think you might soon get a new one.
**Bathsheba** Mercy, how many opinions you keep about you concerning other people, Gabriel Oak.
**Gabriel** Well miss, excuse the words — I thought you would like them. But I can't match you, I know, in mapping out my mind upon my tongue. I hope you'll pardon my blunt way of speaking, miss. Come, give me your hand.

**Bathsheba**  Very well.

*Gabriel takes Bathsheba's hand for a moment, then releases it*

**Gabriel**  I am sorry.
**Bathsheba**  Sorry for what?
**Gabriel**  Letting your hand go so quick.
**Bathsheba**  You may have it again if you like; there it is.

*Bathsheba gives Gabriel her hand again*

**Gabriel**  It's so soft, miss, being winter time too — not chapped or rough or anything.
**Bathsheba**  There, that's long enough. But I suppose you are thinking you would like to kiss it? You may if you want to.
**Gabriel**  I wasn't thinking of any such thing; but I will ...
**Bathsheba**  That you won't! Now, find out my name.

*Bathsheba exits*

*The Lights dim*

SCENE 2

*Outside the kitchen of Mrs Hurst's farmhouse. A bright winter morning, early in December*

*The Lights come up*

*Gabriel is at the door. He knocks on it*

**Mrs Hurst**  (*opening the door*) Ah, good-day, Farmer Oak. And what can I do for you?
**Gabriel**  I've come to ask whether your niece would like one of my new-born lambs, Mrs Hurst. You see, its mother died only last night and I thought she might like one to rear.
**Mrs Hurst**  She might, though she's only a visitor here. She'll be leaving us come St Thomas's Day.

*Bathsheba appears at the window*

**Gabriel**  Oh ... Well, the lamb isn't really the business I came about, Mrs Hurst. In short, I was going to ask her if she'd like to be married.
**Mrs Hurst**  Were you, now? Married indeed!

Act I, Scene 2                                                        3

**Gabriel**  D'ye know if she's got any other young man hanging about her at all?
**Mrs Hurst**  Oh, yes, ever so many young men. You see, Farmer Oak, she's so good looking, and an excellent scholar besides — she was going to be a governess once, you know, only she was too wild. Not that any young men ever come here — but Lord, in the nature of women, she must have a dozen!
**Gabriel**  That's unfortunate. Well, there's no use in my waiting, for that was all I came about. So, I'll take myself off home-along, Mrs Hurst. Good-day, ma'am.
**Mrs Hurst**  Good-day, Farmer Oak.

*Mrs Hurst exits. As she does so, Bathsheba appears from the house*

**Bathsheba**  Farmer Oak, I — I've come after you to say that my aunt made a mistake in sending you away from courting me; she was quite wrong telling you I had a young man already. I haven't a sweetheart at all — and I never had one.
**Gabriel**  Really and truly, I am glad to hear that. Well then, Miss Everdene ... Bathsheba ... I know I'm only an everyday sort of man, but I can make you happy ...
**Bathsheba**  Now Farmer Oak, I never said I was going to marry you.
**Gabriel**  Well, that is a tale — to run after anybody like this, and then say you don't want him.
**Bathsheba**  What I meant to tell you was this — that nobody has got me yet as a sweetheart. I hate to be thought men's property in that way. Why, if I wanted you, I shouldn't have run after you like this, 'twould have been the forwardest thing. But there was no harm in hurrying to correct a piece of false news.
**Gabriel**  That's a terrible wooden story. Upon my heart and soul I don't know what a maid can say stupider than that. Now, tell me, plain and simple, why won't you have me?
**Bathsheba**  Because I don't love you.
**Gabriel**  But I love you, Miss Everdene. And as for myself, I am content to be liked.
**Bathsheba**  It wouldn't do, Mr Oak. I want somebody to tame me. I am too independent; and you would never be able to, I know. Besides, you are better off than I. I have hardly a penny in the world — I'm staying with my aunt for my bare sustenance. Mr Oak, you are a farmer, just beginning, and you ought in common prudence to marry a woman with money, who would stock a larger farm for you than you have now.
**Gabriel**  That about you not being good enough for me is nonsense. You speak like a lady — and all the parish notice it, and your uncle at Weatherbury is, I've heard, a large farmer — much larger than ever I shall

be. Now, I don't want you to make up your mind at once, if you'd rather not; but may I call in the evenings, Miss Everdene, or will you walk along with me o' Sundays?
**Bathsheba** No, no, I cannot. Don't press me any more — don't. I don't love you, so 'twould be ridiculous.
**Gabriel** Very well, then I'll ask you no more.

*Gabriel exits*

*Bathsheba watches Gabriel leave*

*The Lights dim*

### Scene 3

*Weatherbury market square. Early February*

*The Lights come up*

*The various sounds of a busy village market can be heard. A woman sells eggs, a man sells ale from a barrel etc. Liddy Smallbury, Jan Coggan and Joseph Poorgrass are all on stage, either buying or selling farm produce*

*Gabriel enters and starts a conversation with one of the villagers*

*Boldwood enters*

**Boldwood** Shepherd, are you looking for work?
**Gabriel** Yes, sir.
**Boldwood** Where do you come from?
**Gabriel** Norcombe.
**Boldwood** That's a fair distance.
**Gabriel** Fifteen miles.
**Boldwood** Whose farm were you upon last?
**Gabriel** My own.
**Boldwood** Your own? I see. Good-day to you.

*Boldwood exits*

*The market begins to wind down*

*Gabriel sits down, takes out his flute, and begins to play*

*A villager casually tosses a coin in Gabriel's direction as he passes, and exits*

Act I, Scene 3                                                                 5

*There is a subtle Lighting change. It is now early evening*

*Fanny appears. She is hurrying along the street, but stops when she sees Gabriel*

**Gabriel**  Good-evening to you.
**Fanny**  Good-evening, sir.
**Gabriel**  Excuse me, miss; could you tell me how late they keep open the Buck's Head Inn?
**Fanny**  Till twelve o'clock. You're not a Weatherbury man, sir?
**Gabriel**  No. I'm a shepherd, just arrived.
**Fanny**  Only a shepherd? You seem almost a farmer by your ways.
**Gabriel**  Only a shepherd. Gabriel's my name. Gabriel Oak.
**Fanny**  You won't say anything in the parish about having seen me here, will you? At least, not for a day or two.
**Gabriel**  I won't if you wish me not to.
**Fanny**  You see, I'm rather poor, and I don't want people to know anything about me.
**Gabriel**  You ought to have a cloak on such a cold night. I would advise you to get indoors.
**Fanny**  Yes, sir.

*Fanny makes to leave*

**Gabriel**  Since you are not very well off, perhaps you would accept this.

*Gabriel hands Fanny the coin which was thrown to him by the villager*

What's the matter?
**Fanny**  Nothing.
**Gabriel**  But there is.
**Fanny**  No ... no. Please, sir, I must leave now.
**Gabriel**  Yes, miss. Good-night.
**Fanny**  Thank you, sir.

*Fanny exits*

*Gabriel picks up his belongings and turns to leave. Muffled shouting is heard coming from the back of the auditorium*

**Voice**  Fire! Fire! The rick's ablaze. Fire!

*There is a dramatic lighting change and Gabriel's face is suddenly illuminated by the light from the burning rick. There is also the sound of crackling flame, and a confusion of voices, shouting*

*Jan, Joseph and Liddy enter and stand gazing up at the fire*

**Gabriel** *(to Jan and Joseph)* Quick, get a tarpaulin! We must stop the draught under the rick. And a ladder. As quick as you can.

*Gabriel races off to fight the fire*

*Jan and Joseph rush to carry out Gabriel's orders*

*Bathsheba enters. She has just dismounted from her horse and wears a riding habit*

*During the following conversation we hear Gabriel shouting orders to the men at the hay-rick, and we see Joseph and Jan fetching and carrying equipment*

**Bathsheba** Whose shepherd is he, Liddy?
**Liddy** Don't know, ma'am. Quite a stranger by the looks of 'im.
**Bathsheba** Do you think the barn is safe?
**Liddy** Don't know ma'am. D'ye think the barn is safe, Jan Coggan?
**Jan** Safe now — leastwise I think so. If that rick'd gone, the barn would 'ave followed. 'Tis that shepherd up there that have done the most good.
**Bathsheba** I wish he was a farmer here. Do you know his name, Jan?
**Jan** Never heard the man's name in my life, or seed his form afore.
**Bathsheba** Liddy, go to him as he comes down, and say that the farmer wishes to thank him for the great service he has done.
**Liddy** Yes ma'am.

*Liddy exits*

*The off stage noises die down to silence during the following*

*Bathsheba turns away*

**Jan** Did you see 'im, ma'am, sitting on top o' rick, whizzing his great long arms about like a windmill?

*Gabriel enters with his face and shirt smeared with ash from the fire*

**Gabriel** *(to Liddy)* Where is your master, the farmer, then?
**Liddy** 'Tisn't a master, 'tis a mistress, shepherd.
**Gabriel** A lady farmer? Well, I'll be …

*Liddy gestures towards Bathsheba*

Act I, Scene 4

Do you happen to want a shepherd, ma'am?

*Bathsheba turns and she and Gabriel recognize each other. There is an awkward pause*

**Bathsheba** Yes, I do. You can come and see me in the morning. Thank you. Good-night.

*Bathsheba exits with Liddy*

*The Lights dim*

### Scene 4

*The farm office*

*The Lights come up*

*It is now early the next morning. Joseph and Jan are in the office. There is a large housekeeping book on a table. Joseph is reading from the Bible, whilst Jan stares out of the window*

*Gabriel enters*

**Jan** Good-mornin', shepherd; sure ye be welcome, though we don't know your name.
**Gabriel** Gabriel Oak, that's my name, neighbours.
**Jan** Well, Mr Oak, we owe you a deal of gratitude for your help at the fire last night. I'm Jan Coggan. And this here's Joseph Poorgrass. He's painful shy. Isn't that so, Joseph? It's blush, blush, blush with him every minute of the day. 'Tis a' awkward gift for a man, poor soul. And he's suffered from it a long time, ain't that right, Joseph?
**Joseph** Ay, ever since I were a boy.
**Gabriel** But did you never go into the world to try and stop it, Mr Poorgrass?
**Joseph** Oh, ay, tried all sorts of company. My folks took me to Greenhill Fair, and into a great gay jerry-go-nimble show, where there were women-folk riding round — standing upon horses — with hardly anything on but their smocks; but it didn't cure me a morsel. I was just as bad as ever after all. Blushes have been in the family for generations. There, 'tis a happy providence that I be no worse.
**Jan** (*laughing*) So, Mr Oak, how do you come to be in Weatherbury at this lean time of the year?
**Gabriel** I've just arrived from Norcombe — I owned a small sheep-farm there. But recently, I lost all my livestock at one blow. A young sheep-dog

of mine ran out of control, and herded my flock into a deep chalk pit. Two hundred of my ewes died that night, and I was left with nothing, only the clothes I stood up in.

**Joseph** Ye have surely had the luck of Job, sir, and he was a man of great calamities.

**Gabriel** Well, what's done is done. Tell me, neighbours, what sort of place is this to live at, and what sort of mistress is she to work under?

**Jan** We d'know little of her — nothing. She only showed herself a few days ago. Her uncle, Farmer Everdene, was took bad, and the doctor with all his world-wide skill couldn't save the man. As I take it, she's going to keep on the farm. Well, she's a fine handsome body as far's looks be concerned. But that's only the skin of the woman, and these dandy cattle be as proud as a lucifer in their insides. 'Tis said that every night at going to bed she looks in the glass to put on her night-cap properly.

**Joseph** And not a married woman! Oh the world!

*Bathsheba enters, followed by Liddy. Bathsheba sits at the table, opens the large housekeeping book, and takes out a money-bag*

**Bathsheba** Good-morning, gentlemen. Now, before I begin, I have two matters to speak of. The first is that Bailiff Pennyways has been dismissed for thieving, and that I have resolved to have no bailiff at all, but to manage everything with my own head and hands. The next matter is, have you heard anything of Fanny Robin? It seems that she disappeared last night, and nobody has seen her since.

**Jan** Nothing, ma'am.

**Bathsheba** And you, Joseph?

**Joseph** No sir — ma'am, I mean.

**Bathsheba** Well, be sure to give me word as soon as you do. Now, since the death of my uncle, there are certain payments outstanding, I believe. Jan Coggan, how much do I owe you?

**Jan** Ten and twopence halfpenny, ma'am.

**Bathsheba** Quite correct. Now here are ten shillings in addition as a small present, as I am a newcomer. You'll stay working for me, I hope?

**Jan** For you, or anybody that pays me well, ma'am.

*Jan collects his money*

**Bathsheba** Joseph Poorgrass.

**Joseph** Yes sir — ma'am, I mean.

**Bathsheba** What do you do on the farm?

**Joseph** I do carting things all the year, and in seed time I shoots the rooks and sparrows, and helps at pig-killing, ma'am.

**Bathsheba** There's nine and ninepence for you ... and ten shillings.

## Act I, Scene 5

**Joseph** (*nervously trying to thank Bathsheba*) Thank you, sir ... er, ma'am ——
**Bathesheba** Yes, yes — finish thanking me in a day or two. Gabriel Oak, as our new shepherd, do you quite understand your duties here?
**Gabriel** Quite well, I thank you, Miss Everdene. If I don't, I'll enquire.
**Bathsheba** (*holding out ten shillings to Gabriel*) And there's ten shillings for you.
**Gabriel** Pay me when I prove deserving, ma'am, and not before.

*There is a moment's silence*

**Bathsheba** Liddy. Where are the other farm-hands?
**Liddy** Out looking for Fanny Robin, ma'am. Jacob and Laban went off to Little Weatherbury, and William's gone to search for her in Casterbridge. He promised to be back by noon, ma'am.
**Bathsheba** Well, we'll see to them later. (*She stands and closes the book*) Now mind, you have a mistress now, instead of a master. I don't yet know my powers or my talents in farming; but I shall do my best, and if you serve me well, so shall I serve you. I shall be up before you are awake; I shall be afield before you are up; and I shall have breakfasted before you are afield. In short, gentlemen, I shall astonish you all. Good-day.

*Bathsheba exits*

*Liddy follows after Bathsheba and exits*

*The Lights fade*

### Scene 5

*A river-bank overlooked by the barracks. Later the same day*

*The Lights come up. It is a cold, moonlit, cloudy night. In the distance a clock strikes ten*

*Fanny stands on the bank looking up at the barrack windows on the other side of the river*

**Fanny** Frank ... Frank.

*Troy appears at the window and opens it*

   Is that Sergeant Troy?
**Troy** Yes; who is it?

**Fanny**  Oh Frank, don't you know? It's me, Fanny.
**Troy**  Fanny! How did you find me here?
**Fanny**  I asked which was your window.
**Troy**  I did not expect you tonight.
**Fanny**  You said I was to come. You are glad to see me, Frank?
**Troy**  Yes, of course.
**Fanny**  Can you ... can you come down?
**Troy**  No Fanny, not tonight. The bugle has sounded and the barrack gates are closed. We are all of us as good as in the county jail till tomorrow morning.
**Fanny**  Then I shan't see you till then.
**Troy**  How did you get here from Weatherbury?
**Fanny**  I walked some part of the way; the rest by carriers. Frank — Frank — when will it be?
**Troy**  What?
**Fanny**  That you promised.
**Troy**  What? I don't remember.
**Fanny**  Oh you do! Don't speak like that. It weighs me to the earth. It makes me say what ought to be said first by you.
**Troy**  Never mind — say it.
**Fanny**  It is — when shall we be married, Frank?
**Troy**  Oh, I see. Well, you have to get proper clothes.
**Fanny**  I have money. Oh, Frank — you think me forward, I'm afraid. Don't, dear Frank. It's just that I do love you so much. And you said lots of times you would marry me ...
**Troy**  If I said so, of course I will.
**Fanny**  And shall I put up the banns in my parish, and will you in yours?
**Troy**  Yes.
**Fanny**  Thank you, Frank. I know it was wrong of me to worry you, but — but I'll go away now. Will you come and see me tomorrow at Mrs Miller's in North Street? I don't like to come to the barracks. There are bad women about, and they think me one.
**Troy**  Tomorrow, I promise. Good-night, Fanny.
**Fanny**  Good-night Frank.

*Fanny exits*

*Troy watches Fanny leave. The Lights fade*

## Scene 6

*The farm office. Mid-February*

*There is a trunk of old books in the corner which Bathsheba has previously been sorting through*

*The Lights come up. Liddy is scrubbing the floor*

*Bathsheba enters and throws off her hat*

**Bathsheba** I've been through it, Liddy, and it is over. I shan't mind it again, for soon they will all grow accustomed to seeing me at market; but this morning it was as bad as being married. Eyes everywhere!
**Liddy** I knowed it would be, ma'am. Men be such a terrible class of society to look at a body.
**Bathsheba** But there was one man who had more sense than to waste his time upon me. A good-looking man. Upright. Approaching forty, I should think. Do you know at all who he could be?
**Liddy** I haven't a notion; besides, 'tis no difference, since he took less notice of you than any of the rest. Now if he'd taken more, it would have mattered a great deal.
**Bathsheba** Get away, Liddy, or go on with your scrubbing, or do something. You ought to be married by this time, and not here troubling me!
**Liddy** Ay, so I did. But what between the poor men I won't have, and the rich men who won't have me, I stand as a pelican in the wilderness!

*Bathsheba laughs*

   Did anyone ever want to marry you, ma'am? Lots of 'em, I daresay.
**Bathsheba** A man wanted to once.
**Liddy** And you wouldn't have him?
**Bathsheba** He wasn't quite good enough for me.
**Liddy** But did you love him, ma'am?
**Bathsheba** Oh, no. But I rather liked him.

*They hear a carriage driving past*

**Liddy** (*looking out of the window*) There goes Farmer Boldwood. Wrapped up in himself, as usual.
**Bathsheba** But that's him, Liddy! That's the man from the market. He's an interesting man, don't you think so?
**Liddy** Oh, yes, very. Everybody owns it.

**Bathsheba** And who is he, Liddy, this Farmer Boldwood?
**Liddy** A gentleman farmer from Little Weatherbury.
**Bathsheba** Married?
**Liddy** No, ma'am, not him. Never was such a hopeless man for a woman. He's been courted by sixes and sevens — all the girls, gentle and simple, from miles round, have tried him. Jane Perkins worked at him for two months like a slave, and he cost Farmer Ive's daughter nights of tears and twenty pounds' worth of new clothes; but Lord — the money might as well have been thrown out of this window.
**Bathsheba** I wonder why he is so wrapped up and indifferent, Liddy?
**Liddy** It is said, though I don't claim it to be God's own truth, that he met with some bitter disappointment when he was a young man. A woman jilted him, so they say.
**Bathsheba** Oh Liddy, you know as well as I that women seldom jilt men of consequence. 'Tis the men who jilt us.
**Liddy** Did you ever find out, ma'am, who you are going to marry by means of the Bible and the key?
**Bathsheba** Don't be so foolish, Liddy. As if such things could be.
**Liddy** Well, there's a good deal in it, all the same. It makes your heart beat fearful. Some believe in it, some don't. I do.
**Bathsheba** Very well, let's try it. Here, we'll use this.

*Bathsheba produces a key from her pocket. She and Liddy take a Bible from the desk, open it, find the appropriate passage and place the key in the book. Bathsheba shuts it, closes her eyes and concentrates*

**Liddy** Who did you try?
**Bathsheba** I shall not tell you. (*She moves to the trunk and sorts through some books. She discovers a valentine inside one of them*) Oh, Liddy, look what I've found!
**Liddy** What is it, ma'am? May I look?
**Bathsheba** It's a valentine. I wonder how it came to be here?
**Liddy** Why, it's blank. What fun it would be to send it to Farmer Boldwood, and how he would wonder.
**Bathsheba** No, I won't do that. He wouldn't see any humour in it at all, would he?
**Liddy** Well, why don't you toss the hymn book, ma'am? There can't be no sinfulness in that. Open Boldwood; shut ... Joseph Poorgrass!
**Bathsheba** Oh, very well; but it's more likely to fall open. Open Joseph, shut Boldwood. (*She throws the Bible*)

*The Bible lands shut*

Act I, Scene 7

**Liddy** (*delighted*) Now you must write something, ma'am. Something extraordinary.
**Bathsheba** (*having thought for a moment*) I know. (*She writes, speaking slowly*) "Marry me."

*The Lights cross-fade to Boldwood reading the valentine in his office*

**Boldwood** (*muttering under his breath*) Marry me. (*He stands lost in thought*)

### Scene 7

*Boldwood's office*

*Gabriel knocks on the office door and enters*

**Gabriel** Mornin', Mr Boldwood.
**Boldwood** (*hastily hiding the valentine*) Ah, Oak. You've come to do the branding, I expect.
**Gabriel** That's right, sir. It shouldn't take above a couple of hours.
**Boldwood** Thank you, it's good of you to spare the time. Oh, Oak, I met the mail cart earlier this morning and a letter was put into my hand, which I opened, without reading the name. I believe it is yours. Please excuse the accident. (*He holds out a letter to Gabriel*)
**Gabriel** Oh, yes — not a bit of difference, Mr Boldwood — not a bit. (*He takes the letter and reads it to himself*)

*A coin falls from the envelope*

It's from Fanny Robin. She returns the money I gave her. Says she's no need of it now, as she's soon to be married to a Sergeant Troy of the Dragoon Guards.
**Boldwood** Sergeant Troy?
**Gabriel** Why sir, do you know the man?
**Boldwood** Yes, and I'm afraid not one to build much hope upon in such a case as this. He's a clever fellow, and up to everything. A slight romance attaches to him, I believe.
**Gabriel** Romance?
**Boldwood** Yes. His mother was a French governess, married to a poor medical man, but it seems that a secret attachment existed between her and the late Lord Severn. You can imagine what the local gossips made of that. I doubt very much if ever Fanny will surprise us in the way she mentions.

**Gabriel**  I see, sir. Well, I'd better be getting started with the branding, I suppose.
**Boldwood**  Quite so. Oh, Oak I was going to ask you if you know whose writing this is? (*He shows Gabriel the valentine, laughing awkwardly as he does so*) You know it is expected that privy enquiries will be made. That's where the — the fun lies.
**Gabriel**  (*recognizing the handwriting*) Miss Everdene's.

*The two men look at each other*

*The Lights fade*

SCENE 8

*The church. Several days later*

*In the darkness the chiming of wedding bells can be heard*

*The Lights come up on Troy who is standing alone in the church aisle. The chimes fade out and there is silence. The whispered voices of the congregation begin to become audible, although the speakers remain unseen*

**Voice 1**  Where's the woman?
**Voice 2**  She ain't coming, I reckon.
**Voice 3**  (*laughing*) Well, it won't be the first time.
**Voice 4**  And him a soldier, who'd have thought it!

*These lines are repeated, the voices becoming louder and more mocking in tone. Troy becomes increasingly agitated and turns to leave. There is an abrupt lighting change and the voices stop*

    *Fanny appears at the church porch in her Sunday best, with a wedding veil over her hat, and holding a small bunch of spring flowers*

**Fanny**  Oh, Frank, I made a mistake! I thought that church with the spire was All Saints', and I was at the door at half-past eleven to a minute as you said. I waited till a quarter to twelve, and found then that I was in All Souls'. But I wasn't much frightened, for I thought it could just as well be tomorrow.
**Troy**  You fool, for so fooling me.
**Fanny**  Shall it be tomorrow, Frank?
**Troy**  Tomorrow! I don't go through that experience again for some time, I assure you.
**Fanny**  But after all, the mistake was not such a terrible thing! Now please tell me when it shall be, Frank?

Act I, Scene 9                                                                 15

**Troy**  When? When? God knows, Fanny.

*Troy exits*

**Fanny**  Frank!

*The Lights fade*

## Scene 9

*A field on Bathsheba's farm. Early May*

*The Lights come up on Gabriel and Jan who have just taken a break from washing the sheep. As they talk they drink from a flagon of ale and eat hunks of bread from Gabriel's knapsack. The sound of sheep bleating can be heard in the distance. Gabriel shouts off to Joseph at the sheep pool*

**Gabriel**  That's enough now, Joseph. Leave the others in the pen. We'll wash the rest of 'em later.

**Jan**  'Tis a beautiful ale this; a wet of a better class, I call it. It puts me in mind of the old master. Now he was a good-hearted man, God rest his soul, and come sheep-washing he used to let us drink as much ale as we liked. Well, wishing to value his kindness as much as we could, we used to eat a lot of salt fish before going, and then by the time we got to the farm door we were as dry as a lime-basket — so thorough dry that that ale would slip down sweet. Ah, heavenly times.

*Joseph appears*

**Joseph**  (*laughing*) Jacob's been making a mockery of the mistress, pulling her over the coals for pride and vanity.

**Jan**  Oh, I say let her have rope enough. Bless her pretty face — shouldn't I like to do so (*he mimes kissing Bathsheba*) upon her cherry lips!

**Gabriel**  Jan, now you mind this: none of that dalliance talk about Miss Everdene. I don't allow it, do you hear?

**Jan**  (*chastened*) With all my heart, as I've got no chance.

*Bathsheba enters*

**Bathsheba**  Good-day to you, gentlemen. I'm just on my way to Mellstock Farm, Gabriel. I trust I can leave things in your care whilst I'm gone?

**Gabriel**  Yes, ma'am.

**Bathsheba**  I hear that the lambing's been better than ever this year.

**Gabriel**  Yes, ma'am.

**Bathsheba** A good few twins, too, I hear.
**Gabriel** Too many by half. Yes, 'twas very queer lambing this year.

*They see Boldwood approaching from a distance*

Joseph, Jan. It's time we were back working.

*Boldwood enters*

Good-day, Mr Boldwood. Ma'am.

*Gabriel, Joseph and Jan exit towards the pool*

**Boldwood** Good-afternoon, Miss Everdene.
**Bathsheba** Good-afternoon.
**Boldwood** I have come to speak to you without preface. My life is not my own since I have beheld you clearly, Miss Everdene. I come to make you an offer of marriage. I never had any views of myself as a husband in my earlier days, but we all change. My change in this matter came with seeing you. In these last three months, since I first saw your face, I have begun to feel, more and more, that my present way of living is bad in every respect. Beyond all things, I want you as my wife.
**Bathsheba** (*stammering*) I feel, Mr Boldwood — that though I respect you much, I do not feel — that which would justify me to — to accept your offer.
**Boldwood** I think and hope you care enough for me to listen to what I have to tell. I want you for my wife — so wildly that no other feeling can abide in me; but I should not have spoken out had I not been led to hope.
**Bathsheba** Oh, the valentine! Mr Boldwood, I — I didn't — I know I ought never to have dreamt of sending that valentine. Forgive me, sir. If you will only pardon my thoughtlessness, I promise never again to ——
**Boldwood** No, don't say that. You torture me to say thoughtlessness. I never considered it in that light, and I cannot endure it.
**Bathsheba** I have not fallen in love with you, Mr Boldwood — certainly I must say that.
**Boldwood** Miss Everdene, if you will just think for a moment. Should you accept my offer, you shall have no cares — be worried by no household affairs, and live quite at ease. You shall never have so much as to look out of doors at haymaking time, or to think of weather in the harvest. I wish that I could say courteous flatteries to you, and put my rugged feeling into a graceful shape, but I have neither power nor patience to learn such things. I will protect and cherish you with all my strength, indeed I will. Miss Everdene, I cannot say how far above every other idea and object on earth

## Act I, Scene 9

you seem to me. Nobody knows — God only knows how much you are to me ...

**Bathsheba** Don't, Mr Boldwood, don't. I cannot bear you to feel so much, and me to feel nothing. And I am afraid they will notice us. Will you let the matter rest now? I cannot think collectedly. It was very wrong of me, Mr Boldwood, to cause you such suffering.

**Boldwood** Say then, that you don't absolutely refuse. I may speak to you again on the subject?

**Bathsheba** Yes.

**Boldwood** And I may think of you?

**Bathsheba** Yes, I suppose you may think of me.

**Boldwood** Thank you. I am happier now.

**Bathsheba** No, I beg you. Don't be happier if happiness only comes from my agreeing. Be neutral, Mr. Boldwood. I must have time to think.

**Boldwood** I will wait. Good-day, Miss Everdene.

*Boldwood exits. Bathsheba stands lost in thought. A cheer erupts from down by the sheep pool*

**Bathsheba** Gabriel! What was that noise?

*Gabriel appears, laughing*

**Gabriel** Oh, 't weren't nothing, ma'am. Joseph Poorgrass had a slight misunderstanding with a ewe, that's all. Tossed him headfirst into the pool. Is everything all right, Miss Everdene?

**Bathsheba** Yes, thank you, Gabriel. Gabriel, I wanted to ask you if the men have been making any observations on my meeting with Mr Boldwood?

**Gabriel** Yes, they have.

**Bathsheba** Did the men think it odd?

**Gabriel** Odd was not the idea, miss.

**Bathsheba** What did they say?

**Gabriel** That Farmer Boldwood's name and your own were likely to be flung over pulpit together before the year was out.

**Bathsheba** I thought so. Why, a more foolish remark was never made, and I want you to contradict it. That's why I called you over, Gabriel.

**Gabriel** Well then, Bathsheba ...

**Bathsheba** Miss Everdene, you mean.

**Gabriel** I mean this, that if Mr Boldwood really spoke of marriage, I ain't going to tell a story and say he didn't just to please you. I have already tried to please you too much for my own good.

**Bathsheba** I just said that I wanted you to mention that it was not true I was going to be married to him.

**Gabriel** I can say that to them if you wish, Miss Everdene. And I could likewise give an opinion to you on what you have done.
**Bathsheba** I daresay. But I don't want your opinion.
**Gabriel** I suppose not.

*There is silence for a moment*

**Bathsheba** Why, what is your opinion of my conduct?
**Gabriel** That it is unworthy of any thoughtful, respectable, comely woman. Perhaps you don't like the rudeness of my reprimanding you, for I know it is rudeness; but I thought it would do good.
**Bathsheba** On the contrary, my opinion of you is so low, that I see in your abuse the praise of discerning people.
**Gabriel** I'm glad you don't mind it, for I said it honestly and with every serious meaning.
**Bathsheba** I may ask, I suppose, where in particular my unworthiness lies? In my not marrying you, perhaps?
**Gabriel** I have long given up thinking of that matter.
**Bathsheba** Or wishing it, I suppose?
**Gabriel** Or wishing it either. My opinion is, since you ask it, that you are greatly to blame for playing pranks upon a man like Mr Boldwood, merely as a pastime. Leading on a man you don't care for is not a praiseworthy action. And even, Miss Everdene, if you seriously inclined towards him, you might have let him find out in some way of true loving-kindness, and not by sending him a valentine's letter.
**Bathsheba** I cannot allow any man to — to criticize my private conduct. Nor will I for a minute. So you'll please leave the farm at the end of the week.
**Gabriel** I should be even better pleased to go at once.
**Bathsheba** Go at once then, in Heaven's name! I've no wish to see your face again.
**Gabriel** Very well, Miss Everdene. Good-day.

*Gabriel exits*

*The Lights fade*

## Scene 10

*Bathsheba's office. Several weeks later*

*The Lights come up on Bathsheba, who is sitting, reading*

*Liddy knocks and enters*

## Act I, Scene 10

**Liddy** Sorry to disturb you, ma'am, but I've got Joseph Poorgrass clamouring to see you. Says it's urgent.
**Bathsheba** Bring him in, Liddy. I'm not busy.

*Joseph enters, exhausted from running*

**Joseph** Sixty or seventy sheep have broke fence, ma'am and got into a field of clover. They've eaten so much they're already getting blasted. They will all die dead as nits, if they bain't got out and cured.
**Bathsheba** Calm down, Joseph. Now tell me quickly, what must be done to save them?
**Joseph** They must be pierced in the side with a holler pipe made on purpose.
**Bathsheba** Can you do it? Can I?
**Joseph** No ma'am. I can't, nor you neither. It must be done in a particular spot. If ye go to the right or left but an inch you stab the ewe and kill her.
**Bathsheba** Then they must all die.
**Joseph** There is one man in the neighbourhood knows the way.
**Bathsheba** Who is it? Tell me quickly, Joseph.
**Joseph** Shepherd Oak, ma'am. He could cure 'em all if he were here.
**Bathsheba** I told you never to allude to him again. Never will I send for him — never.

*Jan enters*

**Jan** 'Scuse the intrusion, ma'am, but another sheep has just died. That makes seven in all. T'others ain't long for this world either, if you ask my opinion.
**Bathsheba** Farmer Boldwood; he must know something of these matters. We shall send for him.
**Jan** No, ma'am, no. Two of his ewes got into some vetches t'other day and were just like these.
**Joseph** And he sent a man on horseback post haste for Gable ——
**Jan** — and Gabriel went and saved 'em.

*There is silence for a moment*

**Bathsheba** Jan, where is Gabriel Oak staying?
**Jan** Across the valley at Nest Cottage.
**Bathsheba** Joseph, saddle one of the horses; and Jan, deliver this note as quickly as you can. (*She writes a note*)

*As Bathsheba writes, the Lights fade up on Gabriel, who is reading the message*

**Gabriel** (*reading*) "Do not desert me, Gabriel". (*He smiles*)

*The Lights fade*

## Scene 11

*The farm courtyard. The middle of June*

*Jan's voice is heard singing in the darkness. A Light comes up on him singing "Great Things" and on Joseph who accompanies him on the squeeze-box. They remain in one place as the others, dimly lit, move behind them and set the table for the shearing supper. By the time Jan has finished the first verse, the table has been set and the company are all seated around it. The Lights brighten*

**Jan** (*singing*)   Sweet cyder is a great thing,
A great thing to me,
Spinning down to Weymouth town
By Ridgway thirstily,
And maid and mistress summoning
Who tend the hostelry:
O cyder is a great thing,
A great thing to me.

**All** (*singing*)   Sweet cyder is a great thing,
A great thing to me,
Spinning down to Weymouth town
By Ridgway thirstily,
And maid and mistress summoning
Who tend the hostelry:
O cyder is a great thing,
A great thing to me.

The dance it is a great thing,
A great thing to me,
With candles lit and partners fit
For night-long revelry.
And going home when day-dawning
Peeps pale upon the lea:
O dancing is a great thing
A great thing to me.

Cyder is a great thing,
A great thing to me.

## Act I, Scene 11

*Boldwood enters*

**Bathsheba** Good-evening, Mr Boldwood.
**Boldwood** Good-evening to you all. I must apologize for my late arrival.
**Bathsheba** Gabriel, will you move please, and let Mr Boldwood sit here?

*Boldwood sits beside Bathsheba*

Now Joseph, your song, if you please.
**Joseph** Well really, ma'am, I be all but in liquor, and the gift is wanting in me.
**Jan** That's true, Joseph, the gift is certainly wanting in you, liquor or no liquor. And talking of liquor, how about a toast for the mistress of the house? Miss Everdene. Now, as it's the custom at sheep-shearing supper for the master or mistress of the house to give us a song or two, Miss Everdene, would you be so kind as to oblige us?

*The others urge Bathsheba to sing*

**Bathsheba** Very well. Joseph, will you play to my singing, please?
**Joseph** Ay, ma'am.
**Bathsheba** Well, what song would you like? Gabriel, you shall choose.
**Gabriel** Let's have "The Banks of Allan Water", miss.
**Bathsheba** All right, Gabriel. Thank you.
    (*Singing*) On the banks of Allan Water,
    When the sweet springtime did fall,
    Was the miller's lovely daughter,
    Fairest of them all.
    For his bride a soldier sought her,
    And a winning tongue had he,
    On the banks of Allan Water
    None so gay as she.

    On the banks of Allan Water,
    When brown autumn spread its store,
    There I saw the miller's daughter,
    But she smiled no more.
    For the summer grief had brought her,
    And the soldier false was he;
    On the banks of Allan Water,
    None so sad as she.

*There is a quiet, almost reverential murmur of appreciation from the listeners*

**Bathsheba** Thank you, Joseph. Now, don't stint yourselves — enjoy what's left of the food and drink. And Jan, that doesn't mean I'll excuse anyone for a late start in the morning. Good-night. (*She leaves the table and heads towards the house*)

*The others laugh and murmur good-night*

*Boldwood follows Bathsheba*

**Boldwood** Miss Everdene ...

*Boldwood and Bathsheba converse in mime as Liddy gossips to Jan*

**Liddy** That means matrimony.
**Jan** I reckon that's the size of it.
**Liddy** I heard how Farmer Boldwood kissed her behind the spear-bed at the sheep-washing t'other day.
**Jan** Now Liddy, that's nonsense — you weren't even there, so how in Heaven's name do you know?
**Liddy** Well, whether 'tis true or 'tis not, I wish somebody'd kiss me behind the spear-bed — 'twould do me more good than cakes and ale!

*The music starts up again, the accompaniment gently underscoring the following dialogue*

*The Lights fade slightly on the group around the table*

**Bathsheba** I will try to love you, Mr Boldwood. And if I can believe in any way that I shall make you a good wife I shall indeed be willing to marry you. But I don't want to give a solemn promise tonight. I would rather ask you to wait a few weeks till I can see my situation more clearly.
**Boldwood** But you have every reason to believe that then ——
**Bathsheba** I have every reason to hope that at the end of five or six weeks, between this time and harvest, I shall be able to promise to be your wife. But remember this distinctly, I don't promise yet.
**Boldwood** It is enough; I don't ask more. I can wait on those dear words. And now, Miss Everdene, good-night.
**Bathsheba** Good-night, Mr Boldwood.

*The Lights cross-fade to the group around the table. The second verse of "Great Things" is sung as the table and benches are struck*

Act I, Scene 12

**All** (*singing*)  The dance it is a great thing,
A great thing to me,
With candles lit and partners fit
For night-long revelry.
And going home when day-dawning
Peeps pale upon the lea:
O dancing is a great thing,
A great thing to me.

*Everyone except Liddy exits*

**Liddy** (*singing*)  Love is, yea, a great thing,
A great thing to me,
When, having drawn across the lawn
In darkness silently,
A figure flits like one a-wing
Out from the nearest tree;
O love is, yes, a great thing
A great thing to me.

*The Lights fade*

## Scene 12

*A fir plantation on Bathsheba's farm. Late the same evening*

*The Lights come up. It is very dark*

*Two shadowy figures, Bathsheba and Troy, the former with a dark lantern, approach one another and meet. Troy's spurs get caught in Bathsheba's dress*

**Bathsheba**  Oh!
**Troy**  Have I hurt you, stranger?
**Bathsheba**  No.
**Troy**  Ah, you are a woman!
**Bathsheba**  Yes.
**Troy**  A lady, I should have said. We have got hitched together somehow, I think.
**Bathsheba**  Yes.
**Troy**  Is that a dark lantern you have?
**Bathsheba**  Yes.

**Troy** If you'll allow me, I'll open it and set you free. (*He opens the doors of the lantern and casts a light over her face*) I'll unfasten you in one moment, miss. (*He stoops to untangle her dress from his spurs*) No, you are a prisoner, ma'am. I must cut your dress if you're in such a hurry.
**Bathsheba** Yes, please do.
**Troy** It wouldn't be necessary if you could wait a moment. (*He catches sight of her face once again*) Thank you for the sight of such a beautiful face.
**Bathsheba** 'Twas unwillingly shown.
**Troy** I like you the better for that incivility, miss.
**Bathsheba** Go on your way, please.
**Troy** What, Beauty, and drag you after me? Do but look, I never saw such a tangle.
**Bathsheba** Oh, you have been making it worse on purpose to keep me here. I insist upon your undoing it.
**Troy** Certainly, miss. I am not of steel. (*During the following, he continues his attempt at untangling the dress*) I am thankful for beauty, even when 'tis thrown to me like a bone to a dog. These moments will be over too soon.
**Bathsheba** This trifling provokes and ... and insults me!
**Troy** It is done in order that I may have the pleasure of apologizing to so charming a woman, which I straightway do most humbly, ma'am. I've seen a good many women in my time, but I've never seen a woman so beautiful as you. Take it or leave it, be offended or like it, I don't care.
**Bathsheba** Who are you, then, who can so well afford to despise opinion?
**Troy** Sergeant Francis Troy. I am staying here in Weatherbury. There! It is undone at last — I only wish it had been the knot of knots, which there's no untying.

*Troy hands Bathsheba the lantern. She takes it without a word, and exits*

(*Laughing and calling out after Bathsheba*) Ah, Beauty; good-bye!

*The Lights fade*

## Scene 13

*The orchard. The following day*

*The Lights come up. The drowsy sound of bees can be heard. Liddy is in the orchard, hiving the bees. There is a ladder against a tree, a veiled hat, some gloves and an empty hive. Liddy hums as she dresses the hive with herbs and honey*

**Liddy** (*looking up at the sky*) We'll have you caught in no time, you spiteful little b ...

Act I, Scene 13

**Bathsheba** (*off*)  Liddy …
**Liddy**  Beasts. Yes ma'am.

*Bathsheba enters*

Did you bring the veil and gloves, Liddy?
**Liddy**  Yes, ma'am.
**Bathsheba**  Good. Now, I'll climb the ladder; you pass up the empty hive. (*She puts on the veiled hat and gloves*) Liddy, is any soldier staying in the village at present? A sergeant somebody, rather gentlemanly for a sergeant; good-looking too.
**Liddy**  No, ma'am. No, I say, but really it might be Sergeant Troy home on leave, though I have not seen him.
**Bathsheba**  Yes, that's the name. Sergeant Troy. What kind of person is he? (*She climbs the ladder during the following*)
**Liddy**  Well, ma'am, I believe him to be very quick and trim. A doctor's son by name, but an Earl's son by nature. And he was brought up so well — he went to Casterbridge School, and it was said that he got on so far that he could take down Chinese in shorthand; but that I don't answer for, as it was only reported. Has he really come home, ma'am?

*Troy enters and catches the tail-end of this conversation*

**Troy**  He has.

*Liddy is, for once, struck dumb*

**Bathsheba**  Good-morning, Sergeant Troy; I suppose I must thank you for your assistance last night. (*She remains up the ladder*)
**Troy**  Indeed you must not, Miss Everdene. Why could you think such a thing necessary?
**Bathsheba**  I am glad it is not.
**Troy**  Why — if I may ask without offence?
**Bathsheba**  Because I don't much want to thank you for anything. In short, Sergeant Troy, I would rather have your room than your company.
**Troy**  And I would rather have curses from you, than kisses from any other woman.

*Liddy is clearly uncomfortable, and makes her excuses*

**Liddy**  Er, ma'am … I do believe I've forgot to give the cook instructions for tonight's dinner. If you'll just excuse me, ma'am … sir.

*Liddy exits*

**Bathsheba**  Why couldn't you have passed by me last night, and said nothing? (*She climbs down the ladder*)
**Troy**  Because I wasn't going to. Half the pleasure of a feeling lies in being able to express it on the spur of the moment.
**Bathsheba**  How long is it since you have been so afflicted with strong feeling, then?
**Troy**  Oh, ever since I was big enough to know loveliness from deformity.
**Bathsheba**  It's all pretence — what you are saying.
**Troy**  I said you were lovely, and I'll say so still, for by God so you are! The most beautiful I ever saw, or may I fall dead this instant! Why, upon my life ——
**Bathsheba**  Don't — don't! I won't listen to you — you are so profane. I don't allow strangers to be bold and impudent — even in praise of me.
**Troy**  I again say you are a most fascinating creature. But surely you must have been told by everybody of what everybody notices?
**Bathsheba**  They don't say so exactly.
**Troy**  Oh yes, they must!
**Bathsheba**  Well, I mean to my face, as you do.
**Troy**  But you know they think so.
**Bathsheba**  No — that is — I certainly have heard Liddy say they do, but ... (*She catches his eye, and stops in the middle of her sentence*)
**Troy**  There the truth comes out. Never tell me that a young lady can live in a buzz of admiration without knowing something about it. Ah well, Miss Everdene, you are — pardon my blunt way — you are rather an injury to our race than otherwise.
**Bathsheba**  How indeed?
**Troy**  Why, it is in this manner that your good looks may do more harm than good in the world. Such women as you a hundred men always covet. Your eyes will bewitch scores on scores into an unavailing fancy for you, but you can only marry one of that many. Out of these, say twenty will endeavour to drown the bitterness of despised love in drink; twenty more will mope away their lives without a wish or attempt to make a mark in the world, because they have no ambition apart from their attachment to you; twenty more will be always draggling after you, getting where they may just see you; doing desperate things. Men are such constant fools! The rest may try to get over their passion with more or less success. But all these men will be saddened. There's my tale. That's why I say that a woman so charming as yourself, Miss Everdene, is hardly a blessing to her race.
**Bathsheba**  Sergeant Troy, it won't do, your words are too dashing to be true. I won't listen to you any longer. I wish I knew what o'clock it was, I have wasted too much time here already.
**Troy**  What, haven't you a watch, Miss Everdene?
**Bathsheba**  I have not just at present.

## Act I, Scene 13

**Troy** Then you shall be given one. A gift, Miss Everdene — a gift.

*Troy hands Bathsheba a gold watch*

**Bathsheba** But Sergeant Troy, I cannot take this, I cannot. A gold watch! What are you doing?

**Troy** Keep it, Miss Everdene. The fact of your possessing it makes it worth ten times as much to me. A more plebeian one will answer my purpose just as well, and the pleasure of knowing whose heart my old one beats against ... well, I won't speak of that.

**Bathsheba** But indeed I can't have it! How can you do such a thing? To give me a watch, and such a valuable one? How can it be that you care for me, and so suddenly? You have seen so little of me. Please, take it back. Believe me, your generosity is too great. I have never done you a single kindness — why should you be so kind to me?

**Troy** Why? Well, Miss Everdene, I must confess, I did not quite mean you to accept it at first, for it was all the fortune that ever I inherited — my one poor patent of nobility. But upon my soul, I wish you would now. Come, don't deny me the happiness of wearing it for my sake.

**Bathsheba** No, sir. I cannot and will not have it.

*Bathsheba hands the watch back to Troy*

*During the following, Gabriel enters and overhears Bathsheba and Troy*

**Troy** Ah, you are too lovely even to care to be kind as others are.

**Bathsheba** If you can only fight half as winningly as you can talk, Sergeant Troy, you are able to make a pleasure of a bayonet wound ...

**Troy** Miss Everdene, have you ever seen that which you speak of?

**Bathsheba** What?

**Troy** The sword-exercise.

**Bathsheba** No.

**Troy** Would you like to?

**Bathsheba** Yes.

**Troy** And so you shall; you shall see me go through it. I have no sword here, but I think I could get one by tonight. Miss Everdene, if you would do me the honour, at eight o'clock this evening you shall see the most dazzling display of swordsmanship. The hollow down by the mill-pond is a good place for it, don't you think?

**Bathsheba** Oh, no indeed. Thank you very much, but I couldn't on any account.

**Troy** Surely you might. Nobody would know.

**Bathsheba** Well, if I were to, I must bring Liddy too.

**Troy** I don't see why you want to bring her.
**Bathsheba** Well, I won't bring Liddy — and I'll come. But only for a short time. A very short time.
**Troy** Till eight o'clock, then.

*Troy bows and exits*

*Bathsheba watches Troy go, then notices Gabriel*

**Bathsheba** Gabriel! I did not see you there.
**Gabriel** We've just finished in the field, Miss Everdene. The men are taking the hay down to the barns to begin stacking.
**Bathsheba** I see.

*There is a pause*

**Gabriel** Miss Everdene, forgive me for saying, but I wish you had never met that young Sergeant Troy. He is not good enough for you.
**Bathsheba** Did anyone tell you to speak to me like this?
**Gabriel** Nobody at all.
**Bathsheba** Then it appears to me that Sergeant Troy does not concern us here. Besides, he is a well-born, educated man, and quite worthy of any woman.
**Gabriel** He may be well educated, Miss Everdene, but I believe him to have no conscience at all, and I ask you to have nothing to do with him.
**Bathsheba** I happen to know that he is a man of principle — blunt sometimes to the point of rudeness, but always ready to speak his mind.
**Gabriel** Well, mistress, I don't say that he's such a bad man as I have fancied — I pray to God that he is not — but since we don't know exactly what he is, I ask you not to trust him.
**Bathsheba** Why, this is all nonsense, he is as good as anybody in this parish...
**Gabriel** Bathsheba, this I beg you to consider — that to keep yourself well-honoured among the workfolk, you should be more discreet in your bearing towards this soldier.
**Bathsheba** Don't sir, don't. Your lecturing I will not hear. Indeed I wish you to go elsewhere.
**Gabriel** Go indeed!
**Bathsheba** You forget, Mr Oak, that I am mistress here. You shall not remain on this farm a moment longer. You may go.
**Gabriel** That is nonsense. This is the second time you have pretended to dismiss me, and what's the use of it? Tell me, Miss Everdene, how would this farm go on with nobody to mind it but you? Now, I don't wish you to feel you owe me anything, for what I do, I do. But sometimes I should be

as glad as a bird to leave this place — for don't suppose I'm content to be a nobody. No, Miss Everdene, I was made for better things than this. However, I don't like to see your concerns going to ruin, as they must if you keep in this mind. I'm sorry to take on so, mistress, but upon my life, your provoking ways make a man say what he wouldn't dream of at other times.

**Bathsheba** (*after a moment*) Well, Gabriel, you may stay on here, if you wish. Now will you leave me alone, please? I don't order it as a mistress — I ask it as a woman, and I expect you not to be so uncourteous as to refuse.

**Gabriel** Certainly, Miss Everdene. Good-morning.

*Gabriel exits*

*The Lights fade on Bathsheba*

### Scene 14

*The orchard. The afternoon of the same day*

*The Lights come up*

*Liddy and Jan are standing looking up at the hive. Jan has a stick*

**Liddy** Very peculiar, these bees are, Jan Coggan. Our hive ain't good enough for 'em, so it would seem. Ah well, bring it down and we'll try it over in the meadow. Now, I wouldn't tell a soul but you, Jan, but guess who I saw with the mistress this morning?

**Jan** Well, if it was Farmer Boldwood, that's no surprise, Liddy.

**Liddy** No, Jan. Sergeant Troy, of the Dragoon Guards!

**Jan** Sergeant Troy?

**Liddy** He's home on leave, and staying here in Weatherbury. Well, he seemed very taken with Miss Everdene, Jan — very taken indeed! Now, if he marry her, she'll give up farming, I reckon.

**Jan** Liddy Smallbury, how you do talk.

**Liddy** I merely speak as I find, Jan. 'Twould be a gallant life, though.

**Jan** More trouble than mirth, say I.

**Liddy** Well, I wish I had half such a husband, Jan Coggan. Lady Lydia Troy …

**Jan** I don't see what's so very special about him as makes you rattle on like a runaway cart-horse. His being higher in learning and birth than the ruck o' soldiers is anything but a proof of his worth. It shows his course to be down'ard.

**Liddy** He's as fine a man as anybody in this village! He used to be very particular, too, about going to church — so he did.

**Jan** I'm afeard nobody ever saw him there. I never did, certainly.

**Liddy** You're just jealous, Jan Coggan, 'cos you don't happen to cut quite such a dashing figure as Sergeant Troy.

**Jan** Nonsense, Liddy Smallbury, I could've been a soldier too, if I'd wished it, and travelled about the country, all brilliant in brass and scarlet, and impressed all the silly young girls who ought to know better. (*He takes his stick and waves it about like a sword*) I could've, so I could. I just didn't want to.

*Jan chases Liddy off. Liddy laughs as she goes*

*The Lights fade*

## Scene 15

*The hollow down by the mill pond*

*The Lights come up*

*Bathsheba is standing waiting for the sword display to begin. Troy stands before her with his sword*

**Troy** Now hold still.

*The sword drill begins, and Troy deftly demonstrates some thrusts and parries. As he continues the Lights tighten around him, and he begins to move in slow motion. At the same time his voice can be heard as a voice-over. His words, taken from the previous encounters with Bathsheba, are dream-like and sensual*

**Troy** (*voice-over*) Such women as you a hundred men always covet ... your eyes will bewitch scores on scores into an unavailing fancy for you ... I said you were lovely, and I'll say so still, for by God so you are! ... The most beautiful I ever saw, or may I fall dead this instant! ... I again say you are a most fascinating creature ... Ah, you are too lovely even to care to be kind as others are ... I would rather have curses from you, than kisses from any other woman. Ah, Beauty; good-bye...

*Troy finishes the sword-exercise. There is silence and the Lights return to normal*

That loose lock of hair wants tidying. Wait, I'll do it for you.

Act I, Scene 15                                               31

*Troy gently moves the sword towards her shoulder, then suddenly flicks it so that it cuts the lock of loose hair*

   Bravely borne!
**Bathsheba** Why, it is magic!
**Troy** No, dexterity.
**Bathsheba** But how could you chop off a curl of my hair with a sword that has no edge?
**Troy** No edge? This sword will shave like a razor. Look here. (*He nicks himself with the blade and shows her the cut*)
**Bathsheba** But you said before that it was blunt and couldn't cut me.
**Troy** That was to get you to stand still, and so to make sure of your safety.
**Bathsheba** I have been within an inch of my life, and didn't know it.
**Troy** You have been perfectly safe, nonetheless. And now, Miss Everdene, I must go. I'll venture to take and keep this in remembrance of you.

*Troy slowly approaches Bathsheba and picks up the lock of hair. Then he kisses her, gently at first, then sensuously*

*The Lights fade to black*

# ACT II
## Scene I

*Bathsheba's parlour. Late July*

*There are some cases on the floor and a recently discarded hat and cape. Bathsheba has evidently just returned from a journey*

*The Lights come up. Bathsheba stands in front of a mirror, gazing at her reflection in the glass, unaware that Boldwood is watching her from the doorway. She catches sight of Boldwood in the mirror, and turns to face him*

**Bathsheba** Oh, Mr Boldwood, I — I was not expecting visitors.
**Boldwood** What, are you afraid of me?
**Bathsheba** Why should you say that?
**Boldwood** I fancied you looked so. And it is most strange, because of its contrast with my feeling for you.
**Bathsheba** Mr Boldwood, I ——
**Boldwood** You know what that feeling is. A thing as strong as death. No dismissal by a hasty letter affects that.
**Bathsheba** I — I regret that I was obliged to write you that letter, Mr Boldwood, instead of talking to you directly, but I felt that you should know my final decision as soon as possible. My trip to Bath prevented me from speaking to you personally on the subject. I apologize for that.
**Boldwood** Bathsheba — tell me — is it final indeed?
**Bathsheba** It is.
**Boldwood** Bathsheba, for God's sake have pity on me! I am beyond myself about this. I am no stoic at all to be supplicating here, but I do supplicate to you. In bare human mercy to a lonely man, don't throw me off now.
**Bathsheba** I don't throw you off. Indeed, how can I? I promised you nothing.
**Boldwood** But there was a time when you turned to me before I thought of you. There was a time when I knew nothing of you, and cared nothing for you, and yet you drew me on. And if you say you gave me no encouragement, I cannot but contradict you.
**Bathsheba** What you call encouragement was the childish game of an idle minute. I have bitterly repented of it since. Why do you still go on reprimanding me?
**Boldwood** I don't accuse you of it, but I regret it with all my heart. I took for earnest what you insist was jest, and now this that I pray to be jest you say

## Act II, Scene 1                                       33

is awful, wretched earnest. Our moods meet at wrong places. Bathsheba, you are the first woman that I ever looked at to love, and it is having been so near claiming you for my own that makes this denial so hard to bear.

**Bathsheba** I again say, Mr Boldwood, I promised you nothing. Would you have had me a woman of clay when you paid me that furthest, highest compliment a man can pay a woman — telling her that he loves her? I was bound to show some feeling.

**Boldwood** Would to God you had never taken me up, since it was only to throw me down again.

**Bathsheba** I did not take you up — surely I did not.

**Boldwood** Forget that you have said "No", and let it be as it was. Say that you only wrote that refusal to me in jest — come, say it to me.

**Bathsheba** It would be untrue, and painful to both of us. You overrate my capacity for love.

**Boldwood** No. You are not the cold woman you would have me believe. It isn't because you have no feeling in you that you don't love me. No ... you naturally would have me think so — you would hide from me that you have a burning heart like mine. You have love enough, but it is turned into a new channel. I know where.

**Bathsheba** Mr Boldwood, if you would only listen ...

**Boldwood** Why did he force himself upon your notice? Before he stole in in my absence, your inclination was to have me; when next I should have come to you your answer would have been "Yes". Can you deny it? I ask, can you deny it?

**Bathsheba** I cannot.

**Boldwood** I know you cannot. Go then. Go and marry your Sergeant Troy.

**Bathsheba** Oh sir, Mr Boldwood, I ——

**Boldwood** You may as well. I have no further claim upon you. He has stolen your dear heart away with his unfathomable lies. And all the time you knew — how very well you knew — that your new freak was my misery.

**Bathsheba** You are taking too much upon yourself. It is unmanly to attack a woman so. Yet if a thousand of you sneer and say things against me, I will not be put down.

**Boldwood** He has kissed you, has he not? Claimed you as his. Do you hear? He has kissed you. Deny it.

**Bathsheba** Leave me, sir — leave me. I am nothing to you.

**Boldwood** Deny that he has kissed you.

**Bathsheba** I shall not.

**Boldwood** Then he has.

**Bathsheba** He has. I am not ashamed to speak the truth.

**Boldwood** Then curse him; curse him. Whilst I would have given worlds to touch your hand, you have let a rake come in without right or ceremony and — kiss you. Curse him ...

*The door opens and Troy appears*

**Bathsheba** (*after a few moments*) Frank, I am not feeling well. Please show Mr Boldwood to the door. He was just leaving.

*Bathsheba exits*

**Boldwood** Sergeant Troy?
**Troy** That is correct.
**Boldwood** I wish to speak a word with you.
**Troy** What about?
**Boldwood** About a woman you have wronged.
**Troy** I wonder at your impertinence. (*He opens the door for Boldwood to leave*)
**Boldwood** Now look here, wonder or not, you are going to hold a conversation with me.
**Troy** Very well, I'll listen; only speak low, or somebody may overhear us.
**Boldwood** Well then; I know a good deal concerning your — attachment to Fanny Robin. I may say, too, that I believe that I am the only person in the village, excepting Gabriel Oak, who does know it. You ought to marry her.
**Troy** I suppose I ought. Indeed, I wish to, but I cannot.
**Boldwood** Why?
**Troy** Because ... because, Mr Boldwood, I am too poor.
**Boldwood** I may as well speak plainly: I was engaged to be married to Miss Everdene...
**Troy** Not engaged.
**Boldwood** As good as engaged.
**Troy** If I had not turned up she might have become engaged to you.
**Boldwood** Hang "might".
**Troy** Would, then.
**Boldwood** If you had not come I should certainly — yes, certainly — have been accepted by this time. Well, there's too much difference between Miss Everdene's station and your own for this flirtation with her ever to benefit you by ending in marriage. So all I ask is, don't waste your time with her any more. Marry Fanny. I'll make it worth your while.
**Troy** How?
**Boldwood** I'll pay you. I'll settle a sum of money upon her, and I'll see that you don't suffer from poverty in the future. So give up wasting your time about a great match you'll never make, for a moderate and rightful match you may make tomorrow. Leave Weatherbury tonight, and you shall take fifty pounds with you. Fanny shall have fifty to enable her to prepare for the wedding, and she shall have five hundred paid down on her wedding-day.

Act II, Scene 1

**Troy** Well, if, as you say, Miss Everdene is out of my reach, why, I have all to gain by accepting your money, and marrying Fanny. But she's only a servant.
**Boldwood** Never mind that — do you agree to my arrangement?
**Troy** Very well, I do. Fifty pounds at once, you said.
**Boldwood** I did — and here they are.

*Boldwood hands Troy the money*

*Bathsheba is heard descending the stairs*

**Bathsheba** (*off*) Frank.
**Troy** I must now speak to her, and bid her goodbye, according to your wish.
**Boldwood** I don't see the necessity of speaking.
**Troy** It can do no harm — you shall hear all I say to her. You promise silence?
**Boldwood** Yes.

*Bathsheba appears in the doorway in her night-dress*

**Bathsheba** Frank, dearest, are you alone?
**Troy** Yes.

*Troy joins Bathsheba outside the door where the following conversation takes place. She cannot see Boldwood, who remains in the parlour*

**Bathsheba** I'm sorry that I left you with him, Frank. I felt so confused, I didn't know what to say.
**Troy** Hush, my beautiful girl. Don't think of that now. He's gone; there are just the two of us.

*Troy kisses Bathsheba*

**Bathsheba** Frank, it's so lucky. There's not a soul in the house tonight. I've packed them all off — we're entirely alone.
**Troy** Good. Now, you go up, my bright-eyed Beauty. I'll join you directly.
**Bathsheba** I love you, Frank — so much.

*Bathsheba kisses him, and ascends the stairs. Troy enters the room once again*

**Troy** What was I to tell her, Boldwood? That I have come to give her up and cannot marry her? Now you see my dilemma. Perhaps I am a bad man —

the victim of my impulses — led away to do what I ought to leave undone.
**Boldwood** By God, I've a mind to kill you.
**Troy** And ruin her?
**Boldwood** Save her.
**Troy** How can she be saved now, unless I marry her?
**Boldwood** The devil take you, you ...

*Boldwood makes a sudden move towards Troy and grabs him around the neck*

**Troy** Boldwood, give me breath ...

*Boldwood releases Troy*

Well, after that revelation of how the land lies with Bathsheba, 'twould be a mistake to kill me, would it not? Better kill yourself.
**Boldwood** Wretched woman — deluded woman. Take her, marry her, and be damned.
**Troy** But I don't need to secure her in any new way.
**Boldwood** What?
**Troy** (*producing a paper*) Will you read this a moment? That's the paragraph.
**Boldwood** (*reading*) "On 17th of July, at St Ambrose's Church, Bath, by the Rev. G. Randle, BA, Francis Troy, only son of the late Edward Troy, Esq. of Weatherbury, to Bathsheba ... " (*He drops the paper*)
**Troy** Boldwood, yours is the ridiculous fate which always attends interference between a man and his wife. Bad as I am, I am not such a villain as to make the marriage or misery of any woman a matter of huckster and sale. Now, you say you love Bathsheba; yet on the merest apparent evidence you instantly believe in her dishonour. So much for your love, sir! And now that we understand each other, take your money back again. Take it and be damned.

*Troy throws the money down and exits*

*Boldwood sinks to his knees. The Lights slowly fade. A Light comes up on Troy and Bathsheba, in the bedroom, in a passionate embrace*

*The Lights fade to black*

Act II, Scene 2                                                                    37

## Scene 2

*The farm courtyard. The next morning*

*The Lights come up*

*Liddy appears, followed by Jan*

**Liddy** Jan Coggan, that will do. That's quite enough of your foolery. I've got a deal of work to do, and so have you, I shouldn't wonder. Still, if you're set on plaguing me with your presence, there's two bushels of biffins round by the orchard want shifting. You can come and help with those.
**Jan** Oh, I don't know Liddy, that's thirsty work, apple-shifting. I shall need a little liquid refreshment before I start heaving them around.
**Liddy** I see. So, you need a little something to keep you going through the morning, do you? Well, maybe this'll help.

*Liddy kisses Jan*

*Gabriel enters*

**Gabriel** Has the mistress come down yet, Liddy? Joseph tells me that she came back from Bath last night.
**Liddy** (*embarrassed*) Oh, er ... yes, I believe she did, Mr Oak, but I ain't seen her yet. I've been visiting my old grandfather in Shottsford. I only came back this morning. And there's a houseful of work to do, so if you'll excuse me, I'd best be getting on.

*Liddy exits swiftly*

*During the following speech, Gabriel looks up at Bathsheba's window and sees Troy standing there, his shirt unbuttoned*

**Jan** The mistress did come home last night, Gabriel. I heard wheels pass my door after dark — you were out somewhere, I expect. Good Lord, what's the matter, Gabriel? You look like a corpse.
**Gabriel** She has married him.
**Jan** (*looking up at the window*) Don't take on about her, Gabe. What difference does it make whose sweetheart she is, since she can't be yours?
**Gabriel** That's the very thing I say to myself.

*Troy sees the two men outside and throws open the window*

**Troy** Morning, comrades.

**Jan** Mornin' to you, sir. It should be a beautiful one, I reckon. (*To Gabriel*) Ain't you going to answer him, Gabriel? I'd say good-morning, and keep the man civil.
**Gabriel** Good-morning, Sergeant Troy.
**Troy** A rambling, gloomy house this; I feel like new wine in an old bottle here. I am for making this place more modern, that we may be cheerful whilst we can.
**Gabriel** It would be a pity, I think.
**Troy** Nonsense. What this house needs is a bit of life; else we'll all go mad. Which reminds me, Coggan, do you know if insanity has ever appeared in Mr Boldwood's family?
**Jan** Well, I don't know the rights of it, but I once heard that an uncle of his was queer in the head. Why do you ask, sir?
**Troy** Oh, it's of no importance. Well, I shall be down in the fields with you some time this week; but I have a few matters to attend to first. So good-day to you. We shall, of course, keep on friendly terms. I'm not a proud man: nobody is ever able to say that of Sergeant Troy. So, here's half a crown to drink my health. (*He throws down a coin which falls at Gabriel's feet*)

*Gabriel ignores the coin*

**Jan** (*picking up the coin*) Thank you, sir.

*Troy closes the window*

**Gabriel** You keep it, Jan. As for me, I'll do without gifts from him.
**Jan** Don't show too much, Gabe, for mark my words, he'll buy his discharge and be our master here. Therefore 'tis well to say "friend" outwardly, though you say "troublehouse" within.
**Gabriel** Well, perhaps it is best to be silent: but I can't go further than that. I can't flatter, and if my place here is only to be kept by smoothing him down, my place must be lost.

*Gabriel exits*

*The Lights fade*

## Scene 3

*Outside the barn. Late August*

*The Lights come up*

*It is now early evening. There is music (fiddle and squeeze-box) in the background, and the sound of laughter coming from the barn. The harvest party is in full swing*

*Fanny appears. She is dressed in shabby, unkempt clothes, and her face is drawn and pale. She looks furtively about her and takes out a piece of bread which she has just stolen from the farmhouse*

*Troy and Bathsheba appear from the direction of the party. As she hears their voices, Fanny creeps into a corner and hides*

**Bathsheba** Frank, don't give it to them — please. It will only do them harm. They're none of them used to that sort of liquor — and anyway, they've already had enough of everything.

**Troy** You worry too much, Beauty: let me be the judge of this. In any case, it is a special occasion. Why shouldn't they enjoy themselves for a change?

*Fanny coughs and tries to suppress the sound. Bathsheba and Troy hear it, however*

Who's that? Who's there?

*Troy and Bathsheba approach Fanny*

**Bathsheba** *(catching sight of Fanny's face)*. Oh, the poor thing!
**Troy** What are you doing here, girl?
**Fanny** Please sir, do you know what time Casterbridge Union-house closes at night?
**Troy** *(recognizing her voice)* I — I don't know. *(To Bathsheba)* I'll see to the woman. Bathsheba, you return to the barn.
**Bathsheba** But Frank ——
**Troy** I said I'll see to this.

*Bathsheba exits*

Fanny, how on earth did you come here? I thought you were miles away. Why didn't you write to me?
**Fanny** I feared to.

**Troy** Have you any money?
**Fanny** None.
**Troy** Good God — I wish I had more to give you! This is every farthing I have left. I have none but what my wife gives me, and I can hardly ask her now.
**Fanny** Your wife?

*There is a pause, during which there is a burst of laughter from the revellers at the party*

**Troy** Yes. Now listen, Fanny, where are you going tonight? Casterbridge Union, did you say?
**Fanny** Yes; I thought to go there.
**Troy** But Fanny, that's miles from here. How will you get there?
**Fanny** I'll manage.
**Troy** No, you shan't go there: yet wait. Yes, perhaps for tonight; I can do nothing better, I'm afraid. Sleep there tonight, and stay there tomorrow. On Monday morning, at ten o'clock, meet me on Grey's Bridge, just out of the town. I'll bring all the money I can. You shan't want — I'll see to that, Fanny; then I'll get you a lodging somewhere. Goodbye till then.
**Fanny** Goodbye, Frank.

*Fanny exits*

*The revellers can be heard approaching from the barn*

*Bathsheba, Jan, Joseph, Liddy and Gabriel enter. Jan is playing a fiddle, and Joseph accompanies him on the squeeze-box. Liddy carries a bottle*

*Troy grabs the bottle from Liddy. The episode with Fanny has clearly unsettled him, and he throws himself recklessly into the party atmosphere in an attempt to erase her from his mind*

**Jan** Now, ma'am, and no offences I hope, I ask what dance you would like next?
**Bathsheba** Really, it makes no difference.
**Jan** Then, I'll venture to name that the right and proper thing is "The Soldier's Joy".
**Troy** Before you give us your tune, Jan, I must just say a few words to you all. Friends; it is not only the harvest home that we are celebrating tonight; this is also a Wedding Feast. A short time ago I had the happiness to lead to the altar your mistress, and not until now have we been able to give any public flourish to the event in Weatherbury. That it may be thoroughly well

## Act II, Scene 3

done, and that you may go happy to bed, I have ordered some bottles of brandy to be brought to the barn. A treble-strong goblet will be handed round to everyone. And if any of you show the white feather, mind you look elsewhere for a winter's work.

*Bathsheba remains silent, but looks angrily at Troy*

And now, Jan, let's have your "Soldier's Joy".

*Jan starts to play. The revellers dance in a circle around the newly-weds, then exit into the barn*

**Troy** This is supposed to be a celebration. Do try to enjoy yourself a little. Why, Bathsheba, you have lost all the pluck and sauciness you formerly had. Upon my life, if I had known what a chicken-hearted creature you were under all your boldness, I'd never have ——
**Bathsheba** Who was she, Frank?
**Troy** What are you talking about?
**Bathsheba** Do you know who that woman was?
**Troy** I do.
**Bathsheba** I thought so. Who is she?
**Troy** Nothing to either of us. I know her by sight.
**Bathsheba** What is her name?
**Troy** How the devil should I know.
**Bathsheba** I think you do.
**Troy** Think what you will, and be damned ...

*Gabriel enters*

**Gabriel** Excuse me, Sergeant Troy; ma'am. I'm sorry to bother you, sir, but may I have a word in private?
**Bathsheba** Certainly, Gabriel. I was just leaving anyway.

*Bathsheba exits*

**Gabriel** I just wanted to tell you that a heavy rain is sure to fall soon, and that something should be done to protect the ricks.
**Troy** Oh Gabriel, do you never stop? Can't you forget the farm for one evening, and enjoy yourself? It will not rain tonight, I'm convinced of that. Now, pour yourself a drink, and stop bothering me.

*Troy exits into the barn. Joseph enters from it*

**Gabriel** Joseph! Where's the thatching-beetle and the rick-stick and spars?
**Joseph** Under the staddles, most likely. But come on into the barn, Gabriel, there's a pretty tipple just waiting for us inside. Now, too much liquor is bad, and leads us to that horned man in the smoky house; but after all, many people haven't the gift of enjoying a wet, and since we be highly favoured with a power that way, we should make the most of it.

*Joseph exits*

*Gabriel looks anxiously up at the sky, and dashes off in the opposite direction*

*The Lights fade to black*

*There is a distant roar of thunder, and a few seconds later a fork of lightning illuminates the stage*

## Scene 4

*The farm. Later the same night*

*The Lights come up. Gabriel is standing on a ladder, swiftly and deftly thatching the top of a rick. There are sheaves of barley lying scattered on the ground below. From time to time his work is illuminated by a flash of lightning*

*Bathsheba appears from the house, a shawl thrown hastily over her shoulders*

**Bathsheba** Who is there?
**Gabriel** Is that you, ma'am?
**Bathsheba** Oh Gabriel, the storm awoke me, and I thought of the corn. Can we save it, do you think? I cannot find my husband. Is he with you?
**Gabriel** He's not here.
**Bathsheba** Do you know where he is?
**Gabriel** Asleep in the barn.
**Bathsheba** He promised me that the stacks would be covered. Is there anything I can do to help? Surely I can do something?
**Gabriel** You can pass up some reed-sheaves to me, ma'am. Every moment is precious now.
**Bathsheba** I'll do anything.
**Gabriel** The wheat-stacks are covered already, I've seen to that.

## Act II, Scene 4

*Bathsheba takes a sheaf on her shoulder, ascends the ladder, and passes it to Gabriel. She then climbs down, picks up another sheaf and ascends once again. Having passed the sheaf to Gabriel, she is about to climb down when a huge clap of thunder deafens them both. Almost simultaneously there is a bright flash of lightning, much closer than before*

**Gabriel** Best climb down, ma'am. We've had a narrow escape. That fork of lightning was just a little too close for comfort.

*They both descend*

**Bathsheba** Oh, where are the others, Gabriel?
**Gabriel** They would have been here if they could.
**Bathsheba** Oh, I know it all — all. They are asleep in the barn, in a drunken haze, and my husband among them.
**Gabriel** I think they are, ma'am. Well, the storm seems to be passing us by now, at any rate. I cannot understand no rain falling, though. But Heaven be praised, it is all the better for us.
**Bathsheba** Gabriel, you are kinder than I deserve.
**Gabriel** Well, I'd best go back up and finish the job. Who knows if the storm'll return tonight.
**Bathsheba** Gabriel.
**Gabriel** Yes, mistress.
**Bathsheba** I suppose you thought that when I went to Bath that time it was on purpose to be married.
**Gabriel** I did at last — not at first.
**Bathsheba** And the others thought so too?
**Gabriel** Yes.
**Bathsheba** And you blamed me for it?
**Gabriel** Well — perhaps.
**Bathsheba** I thought so. Now, I care a little for your good opinion, and I wanted to explain something — I have longed to do it ever since I returned, and you looked so gravely at me. I went to Bath that night in the full intention of breaking off my engagement to Mr Troy. It was owing to circumstances which occurred after I got there that — that we were married. Well, I was alone in a strange city, and I realized, too late, that scandal might seize hold of me for meeting him alone in that way. And I resolved to leave there, at once, when he suddenly said he had that day seen a woman more beautiful than I, and that his constancy could not be counted on unless I at once became his. And being grieved and troubled, torn between jealousy and distraction, I ... I married him.

*Gabriel is silent*

And now I don't wish for a single remark from you upon the subject — indeed I forbid it. Well, come along, Gabriel, we've work to do.
**Gabriel** No, ma'am. I think you had better go indoors now, you are tired. I can finish the rest alone.
**Bathsheba** Thank you for your devotion, a thousand times, Gabriel. Goodnight — I know you are doing your very best for me.

*Bathsheba returns to the house*

*Gabriel slowly and wearily ascends the ladder once more. The Lights fade*

*In the darkness the sound of incessant, driving rain can be heard*

### Scene 5

*The mill-pond. The following morning*

*The Lights come up and the sound of rain fades away. Boldwood, who has been taking an early morning walk, stands motionless, staring into the millpond*

*Gabriel enters*

**Gabriel** Good-day, Mr Boldwood. How are you this morning, sir?
**Boldwood** Oh, Gabriel, I ... I am well, very well, I thank you; quite well.
**Gabriel** I am glad to hear it, sir.
**Boldwood** You look tired and ill, Gabriel.
**Gabriel** I am tired. I've been working hard all night to get our ricks covered, and was barely in time before the rains came down. Never had such a struggle in my life. Yours, of course, are safe, sir?
**Boldwood** Oh yes. What did you ask, Gabriel?
**Gabriel** Your ricks were all covered before this time?
**Boldwood** No. I forgot to tell the thatcher to set about it. I overlooked the ricks this year.
**Gabriel** Then not a tenth of your corn will come to measure, sir.
**Boldwood** Possibly not. Look, Gabriel, you know as well as I that things have gone wrong with me lately; I may as well own it. I was going to get a little settled in life; but in some way my plan has come to nothing.
**Gabriel** I thought my mistress would have married you. However, nothing happens that we expect.
**Boldwood** I daresay I am a joke about the parish?
**Gabriel** Oh no, I don't think that.

## Act II, Scene 6

**Boldwood** People sneer at me. I've lost my respect, my good name, my standing; lost them, never to get them again. But the real truth of the matter is that there was not, as some fancy, any jilting on … her part. No engagement ever existed between me and Miss Everdene. People say so, but it is untrue: she promised me nothing. Oh Gabriel, I had some faint belief in the mercy of God till I lost that woman. Now I feel it is better to die than to live. (*He remains lost in thought for a moment*) Well, good-morning, Gabriel; I can trust you not to mention to others what has passed between us today?

**Gabriel** Yes, sir. Good-morning, Mr Boldwood.

*Boldwood exits*

*Gabriel watches Boldwood depart, then exits in the opposite direction*

*The Lights fade*

### Scene 6

*Bathsheba's parlour. Later the same day*

*The Lights come up*

*Bathsheba is reading, whilst Troy is idly playing cards. During the scene, he toys absentmindedly with his watch*

**Troy** Bathsheba, could you let me have twenty pounds?
**Bathsheba** Twenty pounds?
**Troy** The fact is, I want it badly.
**Bathsheba** Oh Frank, not for those races tomorrow.
**Troy** Well, suppose I do want it for the races?
**Bathsheba** Only a few weeks ago you said that I was sweeter than all your other pleasures put together, and that you would give them all up for me; and now, won't you give up this one, which is more a worry than a pleasure? Please Frank.
**Troy** The money is not wanted for racing debts at all.
**Bathsheba** Then what is it for? You worry me a great deal with these mysterious secrets, Frank.
**Troy** And you wrong me by such a suspicious manner. I shall suffocate under these restrictions that you impose.
**Bathsheba** I think that I have a right to grumble a little if I pay.
**Troy** Exactly; and the former being done, suppose we proceed to the latter. Bathsheba, don't go too far, or you may have cause for regret.

**Bathsheba**  I do that already.
**Troy**  What do you regret?
**Bathsheba**  That my romance has come to an end.
**Troy**  All romances end at marriage.
**Bathsheba**  I wish you wouldn't talk like that. You grieve me to my soul by being smart at my expense.
**Troy**  You are dull enough at mine. I believe you hate me.
**Bathsheba**  Not you — only your faults. I do hate them.
**Troy**  It would be much more becoming if you set yourself to cure them. Come, let's strike a balance with the twenty pounds, and be friends.
**Bathsheba**  Well, if you must have it, take it.

*Bathsheba hands Troy the key to her strong box*

**Troy**  Thank you. I expect I shall have gone away before you are in to breakfast tomorrow.
**Bathsheba**  Frank, must you go?
**Troy**  Yes.

*Troy accidentally activates the catch of his watch and it falls open, revealing a lock of yellow hair inside. He quickly shuts the watch*

**Bathsheba**  Frank, whose is that lock of hair?
**Troy**  Why, yours of course. Whose should it be? I had quite forgotten that I had it.
**Bathsheba**  That's a lie, Frank. It was a yellow curl.
**Troy**  Nonsense.
**Bathsheba**  That's insulting me. I know it was yellow. Now whose was it? I want to know.
**Troy**  Very well. It is the hair of a young woman I was going to marry before I knew you.
**Bathsheba**  You ought to tell me her name, then.
**Troy**  I cannot do that.
**Bathsheba**  Is she married yet?
**Troy**  No.
**Bathsheba**  Is she pretty?
**Troy**  Yes.
**Bathsheba**  It is wonderful how she can be, poor thing, under such an awful affliction.
**Troy**  Affliction — what affliction?
**Bathsheba**  Having hair of that dreadful colour.
**Troy**  Why, her hair has been admired by everybody who has seen her since she has worn it loose, which has not been long. It is beautiful hair. Why, people used to turn their heads to look at it.

Act II, Scene 7

**Bathsheba** That's nothing. If I cared for your love as much as I used to, I could say that people had turned to look at mine.
**Troy** Bathsheba, don't be so fitful and jealous. You knew what married life would be like, and shouldn't have entered it if you feared the contingencies.
**Bathsheba** This is all I get for loving you so well. When I married you your life was dearer to me than my own. I would have died for you — how truly I can say that I would have died for you. And now you sneer at my foolishness in marrying you. Is it kind to me to throw my mistake in my face?
**Troy** I can't help how things fall out. Upon my heart, women will be the death of me.
**Bathsheba** Well, you shouldn't keep people's hair. You'll burn it, won't you, Frank?
**Troy** There are considerations even before my consideration for you, ties you know nothing of. If you repent of marrying, so do I.
**Bathsheba** I only repent it if you don't love me better than any woman in the world. I don't otherwise, Frank. Frank... just now you said "ties", and then, well, there was that woman we saw last night. Is it hers, then?
**Troy** No. (*After a moment*) Yes. There, now that you have wormed it out of me, I hope you are content.
**Bathsheba** And what are the ties?
**Troy** Oh, that meant nothing — a mere jest.
**Bathsheba** A mere jest? Can you jest when I am so wretchedly in earnest? Tell me the truth, Frank, I am not a fool. I don't ask for much; bare justice — that's all.
**Troy** For Heaven's sake, don't be so desperate, Bathsheba.
**Bathsheba** Once I felt I could be content with nothing less than the highest homage from the husband I should choose. Now, anything short of cruelty will content me. Yes, the independent and spirited Bathsheba is come to this.
**Troy** Talk to me again when you are a little calmer.

*Troy exits*

**Bathsheba** Frank!

*The Lights fade*

SCENE 7

*The parlour. The following morning*

*The Lights come up*

*Liddy sits in Bathsheba's chair, talking to Jan*

**Liddy** "Oh, how I wish I had never seen him! Loving is misery for women always…" That's exactly what she said, Jan, word for word. Then she cried out, as if her poor heart would break, "I shall never forgive God for making me a woman, and dearly am I beginning to pay for the honour of owning a pretty face." Then she bursts out crying all over again. At last she turns to me, very serious and sad-looking, and says; "Mind this, Lydia Smallbury, if you repeat anywhere a single word of what I have said to you, I'll never trust you, or love you, or ——"

*Bathsheba enters. She is on her way out and wears a hat and shawl*

**Bathsheba** Liddy, I shan't be long, I've some affairs to attend to in Shottsford. Jan, you should be helping Gabriel with the fencing in the paddock. You know very well that we nearly lost a dozen sheep last week.
**Jan** Yes, Mrs Troy, right away.

*Jan exits*

**Bathsheba** Liddy, have you seen Sergeant Troy today?
**Liddy** Yes, ma'am. He was up with the lark this morning. Left before breakfast. Said he was off to the races, or something.
**Bathsheba** I see.

*Joseph enters*

Ah, Joseph, there you are. I expected you back long before now. Where have you been, man?
**Joseph** Oh, Miss Everdene — Mrs Troy, I mean: I've just come straight from Casterbridge; there's bad news; about Fanny Robin, ma'am.
**Bathsheba** What's happened, Joseph?
**Joseph** She's dead in Casterbridge Union.
**Liddy** Fanny dead — never!
**Bathsheba** What did she die of, Joseph?
**Joseph** I don't know for certain — she was took bad in the morning, and, being quite feeble and worn out, she died in the evening. She belongs by law to our parish; and Mr Boldwood is going to send a wagon at three this afternoon to fetch her home here.
**Bathsheba** Indeed I shall not let Mr Boldwood do any such thing — I shall do it. Send to him and say that Mrs Troy will take upon herself the duty of fetching an old servant of the family. Joseph, use the new spring wagon and wash it very clean. And Joseph —
**Joseph** Yes, ma'am?
**Bathsheba** Carry with you some flowers to put upon her coffin.

Act II, Scene 8                                                                  49

**Joseph**  Yes, ma'am.
**Bathsheba**  How long had she lived at the Union, Joseph?
**Joseph**  Only been there a day or two. By all accounts, she was seen hereabouts only a little while back.
**Bathsheba**  When exactly did she pass through Weatherbury?
**Joseph**  On harvest night, as I understand it.
**Liddy**  Are you all right, ma'am? You look as pale as a lily.
**Bathsheba**  It's nothing, thank you, Liddy. Now go and see about the wagon, Joseph.
**Joseph**  Yes, ma'am.

*Joseph exits*

**Liddy**  Poor Fanny. You know, ma'am, people used to say she'd go off in a decline; she used to cough a good deal in winter time. It's terrible to think on.
**Bathsheba**  Yes, it's very, very sad. Liddy, what was the colour of Fanny's hair?
**Liddy**  It was light, ma'am; but she wore it rather short, and packed it away under her cap, so that you would hardly notice it. But I have seen her let it down when she was going to bed, and it looked beautiful then. Real golden hair.
**Bathsheba**  We must organize a fitting service for her first thing tomorrow, Liddy. See that she is brought here tonight. The coffin can be laid out in the small sitting-room.
**Liddy**  But ma'am, you're surely not going to ——
**Bathsheba**  Do as I say, Liddy. It is unkind and unChristian to leave the poor thing in a coach-house all night.
**Liddy**  Very well, ma'am. I'll see to it right away.

*Liddy exits*

*The Lights fade on Bathsheba*

SCENE 8

*The evening of the same day*

*The Lights come up*

*Gabriel and Jan are placing Fanny's coffin on two small benches. They do so solemnly and in silence. Liddy stands watching. When the coffin is in place, she puts a small bunch of flowers on the coffin lid, then exits with Jan*

*Gabriel is about to leave when he notices something scribbled on the coffin lid. He takes out his handkerchief and wipes off the writing. He turns to leave*

*Bathsheba enters*

**Bathsheba** Gabriel, thank you for your help.
**Gabriel** It's no trouble, Mrs Troy. Well, I'll sit up and wait for the master, if you like; there's no need for you to stay here in the cold.
**Bathsheba** No, no. You go on home, Gabriel. I'll sit up and wait for him myself.
**Gabriel** Are you sure you wouldn't rather sit upstairs, ma'am?
**Bathsheba** Yes, thank you, Gabriel. I am not at all afraid of Fanny — she was such a childlike young thing, by all accounts, that I'm sure her spirit couldn't appear to anybody.
**Gabriel** Well, in that case, I'll be off home, ma'am.

*Gabriel starts to leave*

**Bathsheba** Gabriel, have you ... have you heard a different story at all ... about Fanny's death?
**Gabriel** *(after a hesitation)*. No, ma'am, not a word.
**Bathsheba** It's just that I've heard rumours; a wicked story that ... But I don't believe it. Besides, there's only one name written on the coffin. Excuse me, Gabriel, I'm tired. I'd like to be left alone now.
**Gabriel** Yes, ma'am. Good-night.

*Gabriel exits*

*Bathsheba slowly walks round the coffin, then stops and stares down at the coffin lid*

**Bathsheba** Would to God you would speak and tell me your secret, Fanny. *(She continues staring at the coffin)* It is best to know the worst — and I will. *(She unties the ropes which secure the coffin lid and opens the coffin. She sees the corpses of Fanny and her child)* Oh God!

*Troy enters*

**Troy** What's this?
**Bathsheba** I must go ... I must go.

*Bathsheba tries to push past Troy, but he prevents her from leaving*

Act II, Scene 8

**Troy** What's the matter, in God's name? Who's dead?
**Bathsheba** I cannot say, let me go, Frank.
**Troy** No. Stay.

*Troy approaches the coffin. He looks into it and sees the bodies of Fanny and the child*

**Bathsheba** Do you know her?
**Troy** I do.
**Bathsheba** Is it she?
**Troy** It is.
**Bathsheba** And the child? Did you know?

*Troy says nothing, but bends down and gently kisses Fanny on the lips*

Don't ... don't kiss her, Frank. I can't bear it — I love you better than she did. Kiss me too, Frank — kiss me.
**Troy** I will not kiss you. This woman is worth more to me, dead as she is, than ever you were, or are, or can be. If Satan had not tempted me with that face of yours, I should have married her. Would to God that I had; but it is all too late. I will live in torment for this. (*He turns to look into Fanny's face*) But never mind, Fanny. In the sight of Heaven you are my true wife.
**Bathsheba** No! If she's that, what am I?
**Troy** A ceremony before a priest doesn't make a marriage. You are nothing to me — nothing.

*The word "nothing" starts to echo from all around Bathsheba and the lighting closes in to focus on her face. There is organ music, ceremonial but discordant, which builds in volume during the following*

*Several dimly-lit figures enter and pick up the coffin. As they take it offstage, Fanny is revealed behind. She is wearing a bridal veil over her loosely-flowing hair*

*The coffin-bearers exit*

*A priest enters and begins to intone a Latin chant (See p. viii). Troy turns to kiss the bride and they embrace passionately*

*The music reaches its climax*

**Bathsheba** (*screaming*) No!

*The music stops. Black-out*

Scene 9

*The following morning*

*The Lights come up. There is the sound of early morning birdsong. The mist is just beginning to clear*

*Bathsheba lies on the ground with a shawl covering her like a blanket*

**Liddy** (*off; from a distance*) Mrs Troy! Mrs Troy! Are you there, ma'am?

*Liddy enters*

Oh ma'am, I am so glad I have found you. Why, you poor thing. How on God's earth did you come to be here?
**Bathsheba** Liddy, don't question me. Who sent you — anybody?
**Liddy** Nobody. I thought, when I found you were not at home, that something cruel had happened. I fancied I heard his voice late last night; and so, knowing something was wrong ——
**Bathsheba** Is he at home?
**Liddy** No. He has not been seen since last night.
**Bathsheba** Is Fanny taken away?
**Liddy** Not yet; but she soon will be.
**Bathsheba** We won't go home at present, then.
**Liddy** But you had better come in, ma'am, and have something to eat. You'll die of a chill.
**Bathsheba** I shall not come indoors yet — perhaps never.
**Liddy** You don't mean that, ma'am.
**Bathsheba** No, maybe you're right, Liddy. It is only women with no pride in them who run away from their husbands. A runaway wife is an encumbrance to everybody, and a burden to herself. Liddy, if you ever marry — God forbid that you ever should — stand your ground and be cut to pieces. That's what I'm going to do.
**Liddy** Oh, mistress, don't talk so. May I ask what dreadful thing it is that has happened between you and him?
**Bathsheba** You may ask; but I may not tell.

*Towards the end of the following speech, the Lights come up slowly and dimly on Troy who is standing with his back to the audience, looking out as if to sea. He slowly removes his clothes*

Oh, Liddy; there was a time, not so long ago, when I was proud of my position as a woman; proud to know that my lips had been touched by no

Act II, Scene 10

man's, that my waist had never been encircled by a lover's arm. And then he came...and he...dazzled me. And I loved him. Yes, I loved him to very distraction and misery and agony. Indeed I would have died for him. It's true, Liddy, my love for him was as entire as any child's. But that's all in the past now. Come, let's go in. It's time to return to the house.

*Bathsheba and Liddy exit together; as they do so, the Lights fade*

*The sound of waves lapping against the shore becomes faintly audible. Troy walks into the sea and the Lights fade on him. The sea sounds fade*

### Scene 10

*Outside. Late August the following year*

*The Lights come up on Joseph and Jan sitting on a bench, drinking ale*

**Jan** Well, Joseph, whatever d'ye think? Gable Oak is coming it quite the dand! Wearing shining boots with hardly a hob in 'em, two or three times a week, and a tall hat-a-Sundays! Why, if he weren't such an excellent fellow, I'd push him into the mud for being so fine.

**Joseph** 'Tis very true, Jan Coggan, he be an extraordinary good and clever man. 'Tis a great thing to be clever, I'm sure; I wish I was, truly I do. But 'tis a happy providence that I be no worse. No, the best thing the mistress ever did was to make him her bailey.

**Jan** And thank the Lord she did! Why, with her gone off for the whole summer, and no one to look after this place the farm would 'ave gone to rack and ruin, so I believe.

**Joseph** And 'e's been asked by Farmer Boldwood to look after Lower Farm.

**Jan** Who's been telling you that, Joseph?

**Joseph** 'Tis blowed about from pillar to post quite common.

**Jan** Well, if 'tis true, I say good luck to him. A toast, Joseph; a toast to Gabriel Oak. You will 'ave another drop?

**Joseph** (*covering his tankard with his hand*) Well ... I've been drinky once this month already, and I did not go to church a-Sunday, and I dropped a curse or two yesterday; so I don't want to go too far for my safety. Your next world is your next world, and not to be squandered offhand. However, for the sake of Gable Oak, I'll drink a thimbleful.

*They toast Gabriel*

*Liddy enters*

**Liddy**  She's here! The mistress is back, so look sharp, both of you!
**Jan**  How is she, Liddy; still the same?
**Liddy**  Much improved, thank the Lord. The change of air has done her a power of good, I reckon.
**Joseph**  She'll be casting about for a new husband soon enough, you mark my words.
**Liddy**  Joseph Poorgrass! Do hold your tongue! 'Tis disgraceful to talk so, and the master not been dead a year. Now the mistress is expecting to see us all up at the house, so come along.

*Liddy hurries off, followed by the two men*

*The Lights fade*

### Scene 11

*Bathsheba's office, a few days later*

*The Lights come up. Boldwood stands staring out of the window*

*After a moment Bathsheba enters. She is still dressed in mourning*

**Bathsheba**  Good-afternoon, Mr Boldwood.
**Boldwood**  Mrs Troy, I ... I trust that I find you quite well after your long absence?
**Bathsheba**  Quite well, sir.
**Boldwood**  Gabriel Oak has been doing a fine job taking care of the farm, I believe.
**Bathsheba**  I do not know what I should have done without him.
**Boldwood**  Quite.

*There is silence*

Mrs Troy, I shall never cease regretting that events fell out as they did. If I said hasty words to you, and showed my feelings too openly, I did not mean to distress you, madam. I was in agony, Bathsheba, and did not know what I said. Please believe me, I meant you no harm.
**Bathsheba**  Mr Boldwood, I too, am very sorry.
**Boldwood**  Mrs Troy, you will marry again some day?
**Bathsheba**  I have not seriously thought of any such subject.
**Boldwood**  I quite understand that. Yet your late husband has been dead for nearly a year, and ...
**Bathsheba**  You forget, sir, that his death was never absolutely proved, and may not have taken place ...

## Act II, Scene 11

**Boldwood** Not absolutely proved, perhaps, but there was circumstantial evidence, Mrs Troy. A man saw him drowning ...

**Bathsheba** A coastguard found his clothes, Mr Boldwood, but a body was never recovered from the water. The fact remains that I may not be a widow. From the first I have had a strange unaccountable feeling that he could not have perished. But even were I persuaded that I shall see him no more, I am far from thinking of marriage with another. I should be very contemptible to indulge in such a thought.

**Boldwood** Bathsheba, suppose you had real complete proof that you are a widow — would you repair the old wrong by marrying me?

**Bathsheba** I cannot say ...

**Boldwood** But you might at some future time of your life?

**Bathsheba** I don't know ... Mr Boldwood, my treatment of you was thoughtless and inexcusable. I shall regret it always. If there had been anything I could have done to make amends I would most gladly have done it.

**Boldwood** Do you know that without further proof of any kind you may marry again in about six years from the present?

**Bathsheba** Yes, I know all that. But don't talk of it. Six years! Where may we all be by that time?

**Boldwood** If I wait that time, will you marry me? You own that you owe me amends — let that be your way of making them.

**Bathsheba** But six years, Mr Boldwood ...

**Boldwood** Do you want to be the wife of any other man?

**Bathsheba** No indeed! I mean that I don't like to talk about this matter now.

**Boldwood** Haven't you been almost mine once already? Surely you can say as much as this — you will have me back again should circumstances permit? Oh Bathsheba, promise — it is only a little promise — that if you marry again, you will marry me! Remember the past, and be kind.

**Bathsheba** Mr Boldwood, I don't love you, and I fear that I never shall love you as much as a woman ought to love a husband; but if you value such an act of friendship from a woman who doesn't esteem herself as she did, and has little love left, why I will ... I will ...

**Boldwood** Promise!

**Bathsheba** Consider, if I cannot promise soon.

**Boldwood** But soon is perhaps never.

**Bathsheba** No, it is not. I mean soon. Christmas, we'll say.

**Boldwood** Christmas. Well, I'll say no more to you about it till then.

*Gabriel enters*

**Gabriel** Oh, good-afternoon, Mr Boldwood. Excuse me, ma'am — I didn't realize that you had company. I've come to finish the accounts, Mrs Troy.

**Boldwood**  It's quite all right, Gabriel, I was on the point of leaving. Good-day, Mrs Troy. Till Christmas, then.

*Boldwood exits*

*Gabriel and Bathsheba watch him leave*

**Bathsheba**  He'll never forget me, Gabriel — never. I fear that if I don't give my word, he'll go out of his mind. I believe I hold that man's future in my hand, and I tremble at the responsibility.
**Gabriel**  I hope that nothing so dreadful hangs on it as you fancy. His manner has always been strange, you know.
**Bathsheba**  But is it right to keep him in hope, Gabriel?
**Gabriel**  The real sin, ma'am, in my mind, lies in thinking of ever wedding wi' a man you don't love honest and true.
**Bathsheba**  But there's a debt, Gabriel, which can only be discharged in one way, and I believe I am bound to do it if it honestly lies in my power, without any consideration of my own future at all.
**Gabriel**  But ma'am, I may suppose that love is wanting.
**Bathsheba**  Yes, Gabriel! Love is an utterly bygone, worn out, miserable thing with me — for him, or anyone else.
**Gabriel**  Well, why don't you ask the parson's advice on how to treat Mr Boldwood?
**Bathsheba**  No, Gabriel! When I want a broad-minded opinion, I never go to a man who deals in the subject professionally. So I like the parson's opinion on law, the lawyer's on doctoring, the doctor's on business, and my business-man's — that is, yours — on morals.
**Gabriel**  And on love?
**Bathsheba**  My own.
**Gabriel**  I'm afraid there's a hitch in that argument, ma'am.
**Bathsheba**  (*smiling, and turning her attention to the auditing*) Now, Gabriel, where were we? July.
**Gabriel**  Sale of two dozen Leicesters to Mr Jacob Tall of Greenhill Farm, South Wessex.
**Bathsheba**  Nine pounds and sixteen shillings.

*They set to work*

*The Lights fade*

## Scene 12

*Bathsheba's and Boldwood's dressing-rooms. Christmas Eve*

*Darkness. A group of carol singers sings. The Lights come up on two areas of the stage in which Boldwood and Bathsheba are each alone, preparing for the Christmas ball. The Lights are brighter on Bathsheba's room for the early part of the scene*

*The carol singers finish their singing*

*Liddy enters Bathsheba's room*

**Liddy** Carol singers, ma'am! I told Charlotte to give them something down in the kitchen.
**Bathsheba** Oh Liddy, I am foolishly agitated. I wish I had not been obliged to go to this dance; but there's no escaping now. I have not spoken to Mr Boldwood since the autumn, but I had no idea there was to be a great party of this kind.
**Liddy** But you will go, won't you, ma'am?
**Bathsheba** Yes, I shall make my appearance, of course. But I am the cause of the party, and that upsets me.
**Liddy** You the cause of it?
**Bathsheba** Yes. If it had not been for me, there would never have been one. I can't explain any more. Oh, I wish I had never seen Weatherbury.
**Liddy** That's wicked of you — to wish to be worse off than you are.
**Bathsheba** No, Liddy. I have never been free from trouble since I have lived here, and this party is likely to bring me more. Now quickly, Liddy, fetch me the black silk bodice.
**Liddy** Oh, but you will leave off that, surely, ma'am? You have been a widow for fifteen months now, and ought to brighten up a little on such a night as this.
**Bathsheba** No, I will appear in mourning as usual.

*The Lights fade slightly on this scene and brighten upon Boldwood's dressing-room. During the following, Liddy helps Bathsheba complete her preparations for the ball*

**Boldwood** Gabriel!

*Gabriel enters*

My hands are a little shaky: I can't tie this neckerchief properly. Would you be so kind?

**Gabriel**  Of course, Mr Boldwood.

**Boldwood**  Thank you. I want it done as well as you can, please. Is there any particular knot in fashion of late?

**Gabriel**  I don't know, sir.

**Boldwood**  Gabriel, I asked you to arrive early tonight in order to discuss something that has been passing in my mind lately; that little arrangement we made about your share in the farm, I mean. I now feel that that share is too small, considering how little I attend to business now, and how much time and thought you give to it. Well, since the world is brightening for me, I want to show my sense of it by increasing your proportion in the partnership. My intention is ultimately to retire from the management altogether, and if I marry Mrs Troy, as I hope to do, I shall ——

**Gabriel**  Don't speak of it, sir. We don't know what may happen yet.

**Boldwood**  But does a woman keep her promise, Gabriel? Or rather, an implied promise.

**Gabriel**  I won't answer for her implying. That's a word as full o' holes as a sieve.

**Boldwood**  Gabriel, don't talk like that. You have got quite cynical lately. We seem to have shifted our positions; I have become the hopeful man, and you the unbelieving one. I have pressed her upon the subject, Gabriel, and she inclines to be kind to me, and to think of me as a husband at a long future time — she has some notion that a woman should not marry within seven years of her husband's disappearance.

**Gabriel**  Seven years is a long time, sir.

**Boldwood**  No, no — it is only five years, nine months, and a few days. Nearly fifteen months have passed since he vanished, you know.

**Gabriel**  Well, sir — don't build too much upon such promises. Her meaning may be good, but remember, you have already once been deceived.

**Boldwood**  Deceived? Never. She never promised me at that first time, and hence she did not break her promise. If she promises me, she'll marry me. Bathsheba is a woman of her word.

*The Lights fade slightly on this scene and brighten on Bathsheba and Liddy. Bathsheba is now dressed for the party*

**Bathsheba**  Oh, Liddy, everybody will think that I am setting myself to captivate Mr Boldwood, I suppose. I dread going — yet I dread the risk of wounding him by staying away.

**Liddy**  Well, anyhow, ma'am, you can't well be dressed plainer than you are, unless you go in sackcloth. And even if you did, you'd still be the belle of the ball, I reckon. Now just suppose Mr Boldwood should ask you — only just suppose it — to run away with him. Now what would you do, ma'am?

**Bathsheba**  Liddy — none of that. I won't hear joking on any such matter.

Act II, Scene 13                                                                 59

There'll be no marrying for me yet for many a year; if ever, 'twill be for reasons very, very different from those you think. Now, come along; it is time to go.

### Scene 13

*There is a sudden burst of music and a Lighting change and Bathsheba is swept up into the midst of the Christmas Eve party*

*Jan joins Liddy on stage; Gabriel exits*

*Boldwood greets Bathsheba and leads her to the ballroom, which can be seen through the door at the back*

*They exit*

**Liddy** No, listen, Jan, he was seen as plain as daylight in Casterbridge Square this afternoon; Maryann told me, and she's never a one for idle gossip. And as for me, I believe it — his body was never found, after all.

**Jan** 'Tis a strange story, Lidd — you may depend upon't that the mistress knows nothing about it. But what the deuce has put it into his head to return to Weatherbury after all this time, I wonder?

**Liddy** You don't need no scholarship to answer that question, Jan Coggan. Here she is with plenty of money, and a house and farm, and horses and comfort — well, he knows which side of his bread the butter's spread upon, that's for sure.

**Jan** You're right, Liddy. If he's alive and here in the neighbourhood, he means mischief. The poor mistress; I do pity her, if 'tis true. He'll drag her to the dogs.

*The music comes to an end, and Boldwood and Bathsheba enter from the ballroom*

**Boldwood** Merry Christmas Jan, Liddy.

**Jan** Merry Christmas to you, sir. (*He looks awkwardly at Liddy*) Well, I'll just be getting us another drink. Come on, Liddy.

*Jan and Liddy exit*

**Boldwood** I am glad to have the opportunity of speaking to you alone. You know perhaps what I long to say?

*Bathsheba says nothing*

Do you give it? The promise to marry me at the end of five years and three quarters. You owe it to me.

**Bathsheba** I feel that I do — that is, if you demand it. But I am a changed woman — an unhappy woman, and not…

**Boldwood** You are still a very beautiful woman. Bathsheba, promise yourself to me; I deserve it, you know I do, for I have loved you more than anybody in the world. So be gracious, dear lady. Give up a little to me, when I would give up my life for you.

**Bathsheba** And you'll not press me about anything more if I do?

**Boldwood** I'll not say another word.

**Bathsheba** Then I give my promise, if I must. If my husband does not return, I'll marry you in six years from this day.

**Boldwood** And you'll take this as a token from me?

*Boldwood hands Bathsheba a small velvet box*

**Bathsheba** What is it? (*She opens the box*) Oh, I cannot wear a ring. Don't insist, Mr Boldwood — don't.

**Boldwood** It means simply a pledge — the seal of a practical contract.

**Bathsheba** I cannot wear it. Mr Boldwood, please ——

**Boldwood** Only tonight: wear it just tonight, to please me.

**Bathsheba** It must be, I suppose, since you will have it so.

*Boldwood takes the ring from the box and places it on Bathesheba's finger*

**Boldwood** God bless you, Bathsheba. I am happy now.

*Boldwood kisses Bathsheba's hand*

*Joseph enters followed by Gabriel, Liddy and Jan. They are singing a Christmas carol*

*Suddenly Troy appears*

*Silence falls upon the whole gathering*

**Troy** Bathsheba, I come here for you. Come home with me. Come.

*Bathsheba says nothing*

Madam, do you hear what I say?

**Boldwood** Bathsheba, go with your husband.

*Boldwood exits*

*Bathsheba slowly moves towards Troy. He goes to take her hand. There is a sudden, deafening gun-shot and Troy falls to the ground*

Act II, Scene 14

*Boldwood appears in the doorway, a gun in his hand*

**Bathsheba** Frank! Frank. (*She kneels by Troy's body, cradling his head in her arms*)

*The Lights fade*

### Scene 14

*Outside the kitchen. March, the following year*

*The Lights come up on Liddy and Jan, who are sitting waiting for news of Boldwood*

**Liddy** I wish he'd come, Jan; my poor nerves are torn to shreds almost.
**Jan** He'll come, Liddy. You'll just have to be patient a little while longer.
**Liddy** They were talking in town this morning about Farmer Boldwood; that he was insane when he did it. Well, if he really was out of his mind, they can't hang him, can they? It seems that he'd been collecting all sorts of things for the mistress — bracelets and rings and lockets — all of the finest quality. And dresses even — silks and satins, each one wrapped in paper and labelled "Bathsheba Boldwood". It makes me shiver to think of it.
**Jan** Well now, Liddy, you can't believe everything you hear in Casterbridge market.
**Liddy** Maybe not; but don't you think he was really out of his mind when he — when he killed the master?
**Jan** I can't honestly say that I do. Oh, Liddy, it would've been better by far if Troy really had drowned at sea — though it's ungodly to say so, I know.
**Liddy** The mistress always said that he couldn't 'ave died that way.
**Jan** How is the mistress? Has there been any change in her this afternoon?
**Liddy** None at all. She's but very little better now than she was at Christmas. She keeps on asking if there's any news, till I'm wearied out wi' answering her. I do hope Farmer Boldwood's life will be spared. If it is not, she'll go out of her mind too, poor thing. Her sufferings have been dreadful; she deserves anybody's pity.
**Jan** (*looking off stage and seeing Joseph returning*) Well, we shall know soon enough now, one way or the other — here's Joseph back from Casterbridge.

*Joseph enters*

Well, Joseph, is there any news? Have the judges made their decision yet?
**Joseph** Ay, 'tis come, at last. He's not to die. 'Tis confinement during Her Majesty's pleasure.

**Liddy**  Thank the Lord!
**Jan**  I say "amen" to that, Liddy.
**Joseph**  Ay, God's above the devil yet.

*The Lights fade*

## Scene 15

*The graveyard. October the same year*

*The sound of distant organ music can be heard coming from the church. As the Lights come up, Bathsheba is seen standing beside the grave where Troy and Fanny lie buried. Behind her, at a distance, Gabriel stands watching her. At last she turns to leave*

**Bathsheba**  Gabriel! How long have you been here?
**Gabriel**  A few minutes, ma'am.
**Bathsheba**  I've not seen you — I mean spoken to you, since ever so long, have I?
**Gabriel**  No, ma'am.

*Neither speak for a moment*

Were you going into the church?
**Bathsheba**  No, I came to see the tombstone privately — to see if they had cut the inscription as I wished.
**Gabriel**  And have they done so?
**Bathsheba**  Yes. Come and see it, if you have not already.

*Gabriel approaches the grave*

*The music fades as Bathsheba reads the inscription*

(*She reads*) In beloved memory of
Fanny Robin,
Who died September 9th, 1847
Aged 20 years.

In the same grave lie
The remains of
Francis Troy,
Who died December 24th, 1848
Aged 26 years.
**Gabriel**  Ten months ago. It seems like yesterday to me.

Act II, Scene 15                                                           63

**Bathsheba**  And to me as if it were years ago — long years, and I had been dead between. Is it true that you are going to take Mr Boldwood's farm on your own account?
**Gabriel**  I had the refusal of it, 'tis true, but nothing is settled yet. The fact is, I had been thinking of leaving here, Mrs Troy — not yet, you know — next spring.
**Bathsheba**  But what shall I do without you? Oh Gabriel, I don't think you ought to go away. You've been with me so long, such old friends as we are, that it seems unkind almost. I had fancied that if you leased the other farm as master, you might still give a helping look across at mine.
**Gabriel**  I would have, willingly.
**Bathsheba**  Yet now that I am more helpless than ever you go away.
**Gabriel**  It is because of that very helplessness that I feel bound to go.
**Bathsheba**  What do you mean, Gabriel?
**Gabriel**  You know how it is, ma'am. People will talk. Say things about … well, about you and me.
**Bathsheba**  What things? I don't understand, Gabriel.
**Gabriel**  Well, the top and tail o' it is this — that folk will say that I'm hanging about here with a thought of getting you some day. Of marrying you, in plain English. You asked me to tell, so you mustn't blame me for saying it.
**Bathsheba**  Marrying me! I didn't know it was that you meant. Such a thing is too absurd — too soon — to think of by far.
**Gabriel**  Yes, of course, it is too absurd.
**Bathsheba**  "Too soon" were the words I used.
**Gabriel**  I must beg your pardon for correcting you, but you said "too absurd" and so do I.
**Bathsheba**  Too soon was what I meant, Gabriel, and you must believe me.
**Gabriel**  Bathsheba, if I only knew one thing — whether you would ever think to love me, and marry me after all this time. If I only knew that.
**Bathsheba**  But you never will know.
**Gabriel**  Why?
**Bathsheba**  Because you never ask.

*The music from the church stops, and everything is quiet for a moment*

**Gabriel**  Marry me.

*In the distance the organ music starts up once again*

*The Lights slowly fade to black*

# FURNITURE AND PROPERTY LIST

Only the furniture and properties mentioned in the script are listed here; further dressing may be added at the director's discretion

## ACT I

**Bathsheba**: hand-held mirror
**Gabriel**: **Bathsheba**'s hat
Barrel of ale
Basket of eggs
**Gabriel**: flute, luggage
**Villager**: coin
**Joseph** and **Jan**: firefighting equipment (tarpaulin, ladder etc.)
Table. *On it*: large housekeeping book
**Joseph**: Bible
**Bathsheba**: money-bag with coins in it
Desk. *On it*: Bible, pen, notepaper
Desk chair
Trunk containing old books. *In one book*: valentine
**Liddy**: scrubbing brush
**Bathsheba**: key
**Boldwood**: copy of valentine
**Boldwood**: envelope containing letter and coin
**Fanny**: small bunch of spring flowers
Flagon of ale
**Gabriel**: knapsack containing loaf of bread
**Bathsheba**: book
**Gabriel**: note written on **Bathsheba**'s notepaper
**Joseph**: squeeze-box
Dining table. *On it*: assorted tankards, plates, bread, fruit etc.
Benches
**Bathsheba**: dark lantern (practical)
Ladder
Veiled hat
Gloves
Empty hive
**Troy**: gold watch with lock of hair inside
**Liddy**: herbs, honey
**Jan**: stick
**Troy**: sword

Furniture and Property List

## ACT II

Parlour chair
Cases
Hat
Cape
Mirror
**Boldwood**: money
**Troy**: coin
**Fanny**: bread
**Jan**: fiddle
**Liddy**: bottle
Ladder
Sheaves of barley
Pack of cards
**Bathsheba**: key
Coffin (lid secured with ropes)
**Liddy**: bunch of flowers
**Gabriel**: handkerchief
Benches for coffin
Bench for **Jan** and **Joseph**
**Jan** and **Joseph**: mugs of ale
**Boldwood**: small velvet box containing ring
**Boldwood**: gun
Gravestone (optional)

# LIGHTING PLOT

## ACT I

*To open*: Darkness

| | | |
|---|---|---|
| *Cue* 1 | Solo flute plays<br>*Slowly brighten lights; forest clearing setting* | (Page 1) |
| *Cue* 2 | When ready<br>*Bring up lights on* **Gabriel** | (Page 1) |
| *Cue* 3 | Melody ends<br>*Bring lights up to full brightness over whole scene* | (Page 1) |
| *Cue* 4 | **Bathsheba** exits<br>*Dim lights* | (Page 2) |
| *Cue* 5 | When ready<br>*Bring up general exterior lights; bright winter setting* | (Page 2) |
| *Cue* 6 | **Gabriel** leaves; **Bathsheba** watches him<br>*Dim lights* | (Page 4) |
| *Cue* 7 | When ready<br>*Bring up general exterior lights* | (Page 4) |
| *Cue* 8 | **Villager** exits<br>*Dim lights to early evening setting* | (Page 5) |
| *Cue* 9 | **Voice**: "Fire! Fire! The rick's ablaze! Fire!"<br>*Bring up burning rick effect* | (Page 5) |
| *Cue* 10 | **Bathsheba** exits with **Liddy**<br>*Dim lights* | (Page 7) |
| *Cue* 11 | When ready<br>*Bring up interior lights; early morning setting* | (Page 7) |
| *Cue* 12 | **Liddy** follows after **Bathsheba** and exits<br>*Fade lights* | (Page 9) |

# Lighting Plot

*Cue* 13    When ready    (Page 9)
*Bring up general exterior lights; cold, moonlit, cloudy effect*

*Cue* 14    **Troy** watches **Fanny** leave    (Page 10)
*Fade lights*

*Cue* 15    When ready    (Page 11)
*Bring up interior lights*

*Cue* 16    **Bathsheba**: "Marry me."    (Page 13)
*Cross-fade lights to **Boldwood**'s office*

*Cue* 17    **Gabriel** and **Boldwood** look at each other    (Page 14)
*Fade lights*

*Cue* 18    Chiming of wedding bells    (Page 14)
*Bring up interior lights*

*Cue* 19    **Troy** turns to leave    (Page 14)
*Change lighting abruptly*

*Cue* 20    **Fanny**: "Frank!"    (Page 15)
*Fade lights*

*Cue* 21    When ready    (Page 15)
*Bring up general exterior lights*

*Cue* 22    **Gabriel** exits    (Page 18)
*Fade lights*

*Cue* 23    When ready    (Page 18)
*Bring up interior lights*

*Cue* 24    **Bathsheba** writes    (Page 19)
*Bring up lights on **Gabriel***

*Cue* 25    **Gabriel**: "Do not desert me, Gabriel." He smiles    (Page 20)
*Fade all lights*

*Cue* 26    **Jan** sings; after a moment    (Page 20)
*Bring up exterior lights*

*Cue* 27    Table is set and company are seated    (Page 20)
*Brighten lights*

| | | |
|---|---|---|
| *Cue* 28 | Music starts up again<br>*Fade lights slightly on table area* | (Page 22) |
| *Cue* 29 | **Bathsheba**: "Good-night, Mr Boldwood."<br>*Brighten lights on table area; fade lights on* **Bathsheba** | (Page 22) |
| *Cue* 30 | **Liddy** (*singing*): "A great thing to me."<br>*Fade lights* | (Page 23) |
| *Cue* 31 | When ready<br>*Bring up dark, shadowy, exterior lighting* | (Page 23) |
| *Cue* 32 | **Troy** opens the doors of the lantern<br>*Bring up squared-off spot to supplement<br>   practical lantern (if necessary)* | (Page 24) |
| *Cue* 33 | **Bathsheba** exits with the lantern<br>*Cut spot* | (Page 24) |
| *Cue* 34 | **Troy**: "Ah, Beauty; good-bye!"<br>*Fade lights* | (Page 24) |
| *Cue* 35 | When ready<br>*Bring up general exterior lights* | (Page 24) |
| *Cue* 36 | **Gabriel** exits<br>*Fade lights* | (Page 29) |
| *Cue* 37 | When ready<br>*Bring up general exterior lights* | (Page 29) |
| *Cue* 38 | **Jan** chases **Liddy** off<br>*Fade lights* | (Page 30) |
| *Cue* 39 | When ready<br>*Bring up general exterior lights* | (Page 30) |
| *Cue* 40 | **Troy** performs sword drill<br>*Tighten lights round* **Troy** | (Page 30) |
| *Cue* 41 | **Troy** finishes the drill<br>*Return lights to general setting* | (Page 30) |
| *Cue* 42 | **Troy** kisses **Bathsheba** sensuously<br>*Fade lights to black-out* | (Page 31) |

Lighting Plot

## ACT II

*To open*: Darkness

| | | |
|---|---|---|
| *Cue* 43 | When ready<br>*Bring up general interior lighting* | (Page 32) |
| *Cue* 44 | **Boldwood** sinks to his knees<br>*Slowly fade general lights; bring up light on* **Troy**<br>*and* **Bathsheba** *in the bedroom; fade all lights to black-out* | (Page 36) |
| *Cue* 45 | When ready<br>*Bring up general exterior lights* | (Page 37) |
| *Cue* 46 | **Gabriel** exits<br>*Fade lights* | (Page 38) |
| *Cue* 47 | When ready<br>*Bring up general exterior lights* | (Page 39) |
| *Cue* 48 | **Gabriel** dashes off<br>*Fade lights to black* | (Page 42) |
| *Cue* 49 | Distant roar of thunder<br>*Lightning* | (Page 42) |
| *Cue* 50 | When ready<br>*Bring up exterior lights; flashes of lightning*<br>*throughout scene* | (Page 42) |
| *Cue* 51 | Huge clap of thunder<br>*Bright flash of lightning, closer than previous ones* | (Page 43) |
| *Cue* 52 | **Gabriel** slowly ascends the ladder<br>*Fade lights* | (Page 44) |
| *Cue* 53 | When ready<br>*Bring up general exterior lighting* | (Page 44) |
| *Cue* 54 | **Gabriel** exits<br>*Fade lights* | (Page 45) |
| *Cue* 55 | When ready<br>*Bring up general interior lighting* | (Page 45) |
| *Cue* 56 | **Bathsheba**: "Frank!"<br>*Fade lights* | (Page 47) |

| | | |
|---|---|---|
| *Cue* 57 | When ready<br>*Bring up general interior lighting* | (Page 47) |
| *Cue* 58 | **Liddy** exits<br>*Fade lights* | (Page 49) |
| *Cue* 59 | When ready<br>*Bring up general lighting* | (Page 49) |
| *Cue* 60 | "Nothing" echoes from all around **Bathsheba**<br>*Close lighting in to focus on **Bathsheba**'s face* | (Page 51) |
| *Cue* 61 | **Bathsheba**: "No!" Music stops<br>*Black-out* | (Page 52) |
| *Cue* 62 | When ready<br>*Bring up general exterior lighting; early morning effect* | (Page 51) |
| *Cue* 63 | **Bathsheba**: "You may ask ... " etc.<br>*Slowly bring up dim light on **Troy** US* | (Page 52) |
| *Cue* 64 | **Bathsheba** and **Liddy** exit<br>*Fade lights on DS area* | (Page 53) |
| *Cue* 65 | **Troy** walks into the sea<br>*Fade US lights* | (Page 53) |
| *Cue* 66 | When ready<br>*Bring up general exterior lighting* | (Page 53) |
| *Cue* 67 | **Liddy**, **Joseph** and **Jan** exit<br>*Fade lights* | (Page 54) |
| *Cue* 68 | When ready<br>*Bring up general interior lighting* | (Page 54) |
| *Cue* 69 | **Bathsheba** and **Gabriel** set to work<br>*Fade lights* | (Page 56) |
| *Cue* 70 | Carol singers sing<br>*Bring up lights on **Boldwood**'s and **Bathsheba**'s dressing-rooms, brighter on **Bathsheba**'s* | (Page 57) |
| *Cue* 71 | **Bathsheba**: "No, I will appear in mourning as usual."<br>*Fade lights slightly on **Bathsheba** and brighten lights on **Boldwood*** | (Page 57) |

Lighting Plot

| Cue 72 | **Boldwood**: " ... a woman of her word."<br>*Fade lights slightly on* **Boldwood** *and brighten lights on* **Bathsheba** | (Page 58) |
| --- | --- | --- |
| *Cue* 73 | Sudden burst of music<br>*Change lights to interior party setting* | (Page 59) |
| *Cue* 74 | **Bathsheba** cradles **Troy** in her arms<br>*Fade lights* | (Page 61) |
| *Cue* 75 | When ready<br>*Bring up general exterior lighting* | (Page 61) |
| *Cue* 76 | **Joseph**: "Ay, God's above the devil yet."<br>*Fade lights* | (Page 62) |
| *Cue* 77 | Distant organ music<br>*Bring up general exterior lighting* | (Page 62) |
| *Cue* 78 | Organ music starts up<br>*Fade lights to black* | (Page 63) |

# EFFECTS PLOT

## ACT I

| | | |
|---|---|---|
| *Cue* 1 | As play begins<br>*Solo flute* | (Page 1) |
| *Cue* 2 | **Gabriel** is lit by the light of the fire<br>*Sounds of crackling flame and confusion of voices* | (Page 5) |
| *Cue* 3 | Lights come up on moonlit night setting<br>*Clock strikes ten* | (Page 9) |
| *Cue* 4 | **Bathsheba**: "But I rather liked him."<br>*Carriage drives past* | (Page 11) |
| *Cue* 5 | Lights fade<br>*Wedding bells* | (Page 14) |
| *Cue* 6 | Lights come up on **Troy**<br>*Wedding bells fade* | (Page 14) |
| *Cue* 7 | Lights come up on **Gabriel** and **Jan**<br>*Sheep bleating; continue throughout scene* | (Page 15) |
| *Cue* 8 | **Gabriel** exits; lights fade<br>*Fade sheep noises* | (Page 18) |
| *Cue* 9 | The lights fade<br>*Sound of bees* | (Page 24) |
| *Cue* 10 | **Troy** begins to move in slow motion<br>*Voice-over; script as p.30* | (Page 30) |

## ACT II

| | | |
|---|---|---|
| *Cue* 11 | Lights fade to black<br>*Distant roar of thunder* | (Page 42) |
| *Cue* 12 | **Bathsheba** starts to climb down<br>*Huge clap of thunder* | (Page 43) |
| *Cue* 13 | Lights fade<br>*Incessant, driving rain* | (Page 44) |

Effects Plot

| Cue 14 | Lights come up<br>*Sound fades away* | (Page 44) |
| Cue 15 | **Troy**: "You are nothing to me — nothing."<br>*"Nothing" echoes around Bathsheba; organ music,*<br>*ceremonial but discordant, building in volume* | (Page 51) |
| Cue 16 | **Bathsheba** (*screaming*): No!<br>*Music stops* | (Page 51) |
| Cue 17 | Lights come up<br>*Early morning birdsong; mist* | (Page 51) |
| Cue 18 | Lights fade<br>*Sound of waves lapping against the shore* | (Page 53) |
| Cue 19 | Lights fade<br>*Sound of waves fades* | (Page 53) |
| Cue 20 | **Bathsheba**: " ... it is time to go."<br>*Sudden burst of music* | (Page 59) |
| Cue 21 | **Jan**: "He'll drag her to the dogs."<br>*Music ends* | (Page 59) |
| Cue 22 | **Troy** goes to take **Bathsheba**'s hand<br>*Sudden deafening gun-shot* | (Page 60) |
| Cue 23 | Lights fade<br>*Distant organ music* | (Page 62) |
| Cue 24 | **Gabriel** approaches the grave<br>*Music fades during following speech* | (Page 62) |
| Cue 25 | **Gabriel**: "Marry me."<br>*Distant organ music* | (Page 63) |

# Great Things

Music - James Clutton (transcribed - D. Gilbrook)

great thing to me With candles lit and partners fit For
Bb  C   Dm           F           Bb

night-long revelry; And going home when day dawning Peeps
Gm   Dm         F         Gm

Pale upon the lea: O—— dancing is a great thing, A
Bb      C        Dm       C

great thing to me——
Bb       C         Dm